ROCHESTER MEMORIES

ROCHESTER MEMORIES

HISTORIC TALES FROM MED CITY

PAUL D. SCANLON, MD

THE
History
PRESS

Published by The History Press
Charleston, SC
www.historypress.com

Front cover, top, left to right: Belva Snodgrass. *Courtesy of the History Center of Olmsted County*; Second Lieutenant Leland Gordon Fiegel (1937) after finishing flight school. *Courtesy of the family of Colonel Leland Fiegel*; Mabel Root. *Used with permission of Mayo Foundation for Medical Education and Research*; *bottom, left to right*: Red Oaks or "Willson's Castle." *Postcard image*; Burt Eaton. *Used with permission of Mayo Foundation for Medical Education and Research*; Monarch Foods. *Postcard image*.
Back cover: Aerial view of downtown Rochester from above Silver Lake Park. *Courtesy of Dean Riggott Photography*.

First published 2023

Manufactured in the United States

ISBN 9781467154352

Library of Congress Control Number: 2023937200

Notice: The information in this book is true and complete to the best of our knowledge. It is offered without guarantee on the part of the author or The History Press. The author and The History Press disclaim all liability in connection with the use of this book.

To revived memories of Leland Fiegel, Henry Wellcome, Luis Alvarez, Maud Mellish Wilson, Leda Stacy, Earl Wood, Alonzo Pickle and others who have become my heroes.

CONTENTS

Contents

CONTENTS

Preface

ROCHESTER REVISITED

More Stories, Less Obvious Origins

My previous book, *Rochester Stories: A Med City History*, was published in June 2021. I wrote it with the intention of recording stories that I, as a Rochester native, have recited repeatedly to colleagues and students during my thirty-five years as a Mayo Clinic physician, often in response to such questions as "Why did they build the Mayo Clinic in the middle of the cornfields (or 'fly-over country' or 'nowhere')?" and others.

My paternal grandfather, Maurice Scanlon, lived an interesting life, and in his later years, he was a great storyteller. Family members used to say, "We should write these down"; however, no one did, and his stories died with him. I wished to avoid that fate for good stories about my home city that are mostly unknown except to a few local history buffs. Examples include the story of Henry Wellcome, the pharmaceutical giant, who became the third-greatest philanthropist of all time, all humanity. He began his career here in Rochester and was mentored and supported by William Worrall Mayo, the father of the Mayo brothers, yet he is mostly unknown here. A similar inexplicable anonymity has befallen Rochester High School alumnus and Nobel laureate Luis Alvarez and quite a few others.

Since the publication of the previous book, I have had many opportunities to meet with book clubs, service clubs and other groups to discuss *Rochester Stories* and to talk about the process of creating the book while promoting some of my favorite stories. There is no such thing as a complete history, and after I finished the first book, I had a lot of stories that didn't fit in 208 pages. I was not sure if the remainder was good enough to justify another book, and I also knew that I would not be able to decide until I had written most of the book. So, I continued writing. In the process, I discovered some new (to me) stories, good stories. Unlike the first book, these are not stories that come up in response to frequently asked questions. Some seemed utterly forgotten. I enjoyed learning them and writing about them, and I hope you will enjoy reading them.

This book follows the format of the previous book—that is, it consists of a sequence of stories written independently, published in chronological order but readable in any order, a single story at a time or in sequence. That format seems to make the book more digestible and the individual stories more memorable.

In writing the previous book, I attempted to present the history of Rochester with enough about Mayo Clinic to inform but not overwhelm with detail. Naturally, some complained that they wanted more about Mayo Clinic. They will be happy to know that my good friend Anthony J. Bianco III is nearly finished writing his comprehensive history of Mayo Clinic, which will be published in two volumes, the first in 2023 or 2024.

Although some people complain that history can be boring, it seems that many residents of Rochester and visitors to Rochester are intrigued by the unique coevolution of Mayo Clinic and Rochester and wish to understand it better. I hope that this book can fill in more voids in our collective memory and provide a fuller understanding of the unique history of this symbiosis. Enjoy!

ACKNOWLEDGEMENTS

This book was written along the banks of the Zumbro River, known as Wapka Wazi Oju (pine-planted river) to earlier inhabitants, the Eastern Dakota (or Santee). In fact, one of their encampments in 1854, during their coerced move westward to a reservation, was less than five hundred meters from here. Their story was told to the best of my ability in my previous book, *Rochester Stories: A Med City History*. We remain indebted to them for their legacy, the lands of southeast Minnesota, also called the Southeast Triangle or Siouxland, in which Rochester sits.

Since the previous book was released in June 2021, we have experienced a smoldering continuation of the COVID pandemic, a burst of inflation, intermittent reminders of the coming violence of climate change, a brutal Russian invasion of Ukraine in February 2022 and deteriorating relations with China. We sit on a precipice with the potential to devolve into World War III or nuclear holocaust. I continue to hope for a just conclusion of the invasion without catastrophic outcomes. I am not optimistic about the consequences of our nonresponse to climate change.

Meanwhile, thanks to you, the reader, for taking a few minutes to read this personal reflection of thanks.

Thanks to readers of my previous book, *Rochester Stories: A Med City History*, particularly for constructive feedback, discussions and new ideas.

Thanks to the Fiegel family, particularly Scott and Audrey, for providing what I consider the best story in this book, the story of Audrey's brother and Scott's uncle Leland Fiegel. Related images are reproduced with permission of the Fiegel family.

Aerial view of Rochester, Silver Lake Park in foreground, site of the 1854 Dakota encampment. *Courtesy of Dean Riggott Photography.*

Thanks again to the staff and volunteers of the History Center of Olmsted County (HCOC), particularly to Krista Lewis, for archival information, photographs and encouragement. The fifteen images from HCOC are used with their gracious permission.

Similarly, thanks to the staff of the Mayo Clinic W. Bruce Fye Center for the History of Medicine, particularly Emily Christopherson, for help with archival materials and for use of seventeen photographs from the archives. Thanks also to Rosemary Perry in the Section of Publications. Images are used with permission of Mayo Foundation for Medical Education and Research. All rights reserved. Courtesy of the W. Bruce Fye Center for the History of Medicine, Mayo Clinic, Rochester, Minnesota. One additional image with Mayo copyright is from a 1940 Mayo Foundation brochure from my collection. It also is used with permission of Mayo Foundation for Medical Education and Research. All rights reserved.

Thanks to Jeff Pieters and Joe Ahlquist at the *Post Bulletin* for ten photographs from the pages of the *Post Bulletin* and *Rochester Magazine*. Those images were located in the archives, scanned and uploaded by Martha Chapin, Susan Hansen and other volunteers at the Rochester Public Library with the permission of the *Rochester Post Bulletin*.

Thanks to my good friend Dean Riggott, of Dean Riggott Photography, for generously sharing nine of his gorgeous photographs.

Two images of work by Judy Onofrio and a photo of her are reproduced with her permission and are copyrighted.

Postcard images are scanned from my personal collection. To avoid copyright encroachment, all postcard images are either in public domain because of age (pre-1923) or are uncopyrighted images (no photographer identified).

And thanks to Virginia Allie for the candid photo of me, printed with the "About the Author" section.

My photographs are copyright, all rights reserved. I hope you find them informative despite their utilitarian quality and composition.

Thanks to my friends and role models as historical writers: Anthony J. "Tony" Bianco III, W. Bruce Fye MD and Christopher J. Boes MD.

Special thanks to Ken Allsen for help with stories and information regarding Assisi Heights, the Heffron brothers, George Healy, Horace Horton, all things Crawford and architecture generally. Thanks for ideas and inspiration to other local historians, including Tom Weber, Lee Hilgendorf, Amy Jo Hahn, Virginia Wright-Peterson and our late friend Alan Calavano.

Thanks to John Rodrigue, my editor, and his colleagues at The History Press, for professionalism, knowledge, skill and cordial interactions.

Thanks to my former colleagues in the Division of Pulmonary and Critical Care Medicine, the Dolores Jean Lavins Center for Humanities in Medicine and the Mayo Clinic as a whole for flawlessly shouldering my former workload when I retired near the end of 2019 and then spending the next year of their lives heroically caring for the sickest COVID patients at Mayo Clinic Hospitals.

Thanks and lots of love to my wife, Maggie; Brian and Marianne; Luke; Kelsey and Jake; our grandkids, Will, Charlotte Tom, Kinley, Ben, Liam and Idris; my mom, Jane; and my sister, Patricia, and her husband, Harrison. They provided support, encouragement and love to me through this lengthy process. I would also like to remember my grandfathers, Maurice and Edwin; my dad, Paul W.; and my brother, Barry, who provided a lot of memories.

I

EARLY DAYS (1854–1914)

GHOST TOWNS AND SMALL TOWNS OF OLMSTED COUNTY, 1855

Olmsted County was incorporated in 1855, Rochester in 1858. The first white settler in Olmsted County was either Jacob Goss in Pleasant Grove Township[1] or Hiram Thompson in Dover Township in 1853.[2] Outside of Rochester, the bulk of Olmsted County is agricultural land. Small cities include Stewartville (pop. 6,120), Byron (pop. 5,462), Eyota (pop. 2,035), Dover (pop. 763), and parts of Pine Island (pop. 3,600) and Chatfield (pop. 2,990). Each has its own history and substantial businesses, rivals Rochester in K-12 education and serves as a bedroom community for Rochester workers. Each has grown in recent years, though not at the pace of Rochester, the fastest-growing city in Minnesota. Unlike typical suburbs, their developed cores are not immediately adjacent to Rochester but sit eight to eighteen miles distant.

The county is divided into eighteen townships, mostly six by six miles each. It is five townships wide (thirty miles east–west) by four townships high (twenty-four miles north–south). Two townships at the northeast corner, Elgin and Plainview, were returned to Wabasha County, from which they came, sometime around 1855. In 1857, a twelve-mile-wide by one-mile-high strip was added to the south border of High Forest Township from Mower County. It has been called the "Panhandle" or "Mile Strip." Of the eighteen townships, ten have a populated nucleus by the same name (Oronoco, Viola,

Contemporary Pine Island. *Courtesy of Dean Riggott Photography.*

Main Street, Eyota, Minnesota. *From* Andreas's Historical Atlas of the State of Minnesota, *1874.*

Salem, Rochester, Marion, Eyota, Dover, Rock Dell, High Forest, Pleasant Grove) while eight do not (New Haven, Farmington, Kalmar, Cascade, Haverhill, Quincy, Orion, Elmira).

Most smaller towns of Olmsted County have lost population, attributable to declining birth rates, urbanization of employment opportunities, consolidation of schools and improvements in transportation. Some towns that showed early promise faded in later years. Oronoco (pop. 1,577), with four branches or forks of the Zumbro converging nearby, had the greatest potential of any town in Olmsted County for water-powered mills. As an acknowledgement of its waterpower, it was named for the powerful South American Orinoco River, though spelled differently. It rivaled Rochester in the 1855 referendum for the county seat but faded thereafter in the shadow of Rochester eleven miles to the southeast. It is an independently incorporated (in 1968) city but is part of the Rochester School District. Similarly, Marion (unincorporated) was an early rival that faded. High Forest (unincorporated), the namesake village of High Forest Township and the birthplace of painter Nicholas Brewer (see pages 33–34), was once a bustling town with a mill, a blacksmith, two stores, a tavern, two churches[3] and the Hotel Tattersall (kitchen, dining room, post office, saloon on first floor, five guest rooms on the second floor and ballroom on the third floor).[4] However, Charles Stewart settled three miles to the east in 1857 and built his mill the following year, creating Lake Alice (later called Lake Florence) and Stewartville. In 1890, the Winona and Southwestern Railroad built its station in Stewartville rather than High Forest, after which Stewartville grew rapidly while High Forest dwindled to a mere road crossing village of two dozen homesteads with a church and cemetery.[5]

The villages of Chester, Cummingsville, Danesville, Douglas, Genoa, Pleasant Grove, Potsdam, Predmore, Rock Dell, Salem Corners, Simpson and Viola are all either unincorporated or minor civil divisions (MCDs) of Olmsted County. They do not have a census aside from those of the surrounding townships. They no longer have their country school, post office or grocery store, which most had at one time. Each has up to a few dozen homes, and most have one or more commercial establishments or a church. The inhabitants self-select a quieter life away from the city. The commute to Rochester is twenty-five minutes or less.

Douglas was named for Harrison Douglass, who arrived in the spring of 1855, was the first blacksmith in Olmsted County, farmed in the area and built the grain elevator at Douglass Station in 1878.[6] No one knows what happened to the second *s*. The village was once known as Center Grove.[7]

Discarded names are not uncommon. Eyota Township was originally called Springfield in 1858 but was renamed the following year with the Dakota word for "greatest." Curiously, its post office was called Greenfield from 1857 until 1864. Other name changes include Bear Grove to Byron, Whitewater to Dover Center to Dover, Finley to Marion, Durango to New Haven, Curtis to Pleasant Grove, Lexington to Salem to Salem Corners, Groesbeck to Simpson,[8] Washington to Viola and Zumbro to Grant to Sherman to Haverhill. There is another Genoa (also unincorporated) in St. Louis County.

The Viola Gopher Count, founded in 1874, is an annual celebration with a competition for the most trapped gophers (the mascot of the University of Minnesota) among local citizens, judged by the number of gopher forepaws submitted for bounty. It is said to be the second-longest-running community event in the United States (after the Kentucky Derby). *Spy* magazine described it as "what may be the single most appalling annual event held in the country."[9]

Little Valley in Quincy Township had a post office from 1863 to 1902. Farm Hill in Farmington Township had a post office from 1863 to 1889. Ringe, also in Farmington Township, had a post office from 1898 to 1902. Othello, in New Haven Township, had a post office from 1862 to 1902. Each village had one or more country schools, of which Olmsted County had over one hundred. Today, all that remains of each village is a country cemetery dating from the 1860s to the 1880s, making them literally ghost towns.[10]

Some towns fared worse. Durango was founded in 1856 at what is now the intersection of County Roads 12 and 3, three and a half miles west of the Oronoco exit (100th Street) from U.S. Highway 52 north of Rochester. Two years later, New Haven Township was named for New Haven, Connecticut, and Durango was renamed New Haven. Initially, it had a store and a mill, and it had a post office until 1905. For unclear reasons (probably related to the routing of the Chicago and Great Western Railroad closer to Oronoco), the town dwindled. The township hall was built a mile to the southeast, and there are only a few houses today at the intersection with no sign of the old village.

Plank's Crossing, Laird and Horton were adjacent railroad station villages in Eyota Township (Chicago and North Western and Chicago and Great Western times two, respectively) within a mile of each other. Laird had a tavern and a post office from 1891 to 1905, and Horton had a post office from 1892 to 1905. None of the names survived. The adjacent cemetery is called Cline Cemetery for the family on whose farm it is located. Oak Grove and Holy Redeemer Cemeteries are also nearby.

Othello Cemetery. *Photo by Paul David Scanlon.*

Judge School. *Photo by Paul David Scanlon.*

Carrollville, at the west end of the conjoint portion of County Roads 16 and 20 (a mile west of St. Bridget's Church), had a post office from 1872 to 1902 and a school. The abandoned school still stands. The village of Olmsted was created as a railroad station and siding for the Winona and St. Peter Railroad in 1870. Just four and a half miles west of Rochester, its location was just north of U.S. 14 and west of County Road 44 (60th Avenue W). It had a post office, a warehouse, a store and a school. It was abandoned after five years, and nothing remains.[11]

The village of Judge was established in 1891 as a stop for the Winona and Southwestern (later the Chicago and Great Western) Railroad, midway along the six-mile route from Stewartville to Simpson on the way to Rochester. A village was created at what is now 85th Street SE just east of U.S. 63 on the farm of Edward Judge, for whom the village was named. It had an elevator and a store and a post office from 1897 to 1902. Mr. Judge died in 1904, and train service eventually ceased. Judge School welcomed children from 1906 until consolidation in 1957. It stands eerily abandoned in an overgrown lot on 80th Street South. The Judge house and store burned in 1940, leaving no other trace of the village. Even the old railroad track bed is difficult to discern, barely visible south of 85th Street.

MILLS, 1855

In the days before the availability of electricity, water-powered mills of various types were important to the production of basic staples. Rochester was a center for wheat production. Unlike Minneapolis, it is not rich in waterpower but has enough to provide for some milling. There were several mill sites within Rochester in the early days. The mills went by several names as they evolved over time.

Joseph Alexander acquired rights to the waterpower of Bear Creek in southeast Rochester in 1855. In partnership with W. Goldsworthy, he built a lumber mill and furniture factory that burned down in 1863. In 1872, Alexander partnered with W.G. Bartley to build Rochester's first woolen mill on Bear Creek. (The mill was near the north end of what is now Slatterly Park, between Rochester Street [6th Street SE] and College Street [4th Street SE]].) The dam for the mills was located about one block upstream between 7th and 8th Streets. A plaque along the bike path commemorates the mill. "The mill operated 7 months of the year, processing 100 pounds of wool per day to produce blankets, flannel, stockings and yarn. Alexander and Bartley sold their woolen goods from a store on Broadway. By 1880, Alexander had become sole owner of the woolen mill. Alexander converted the mill to operate on steam power sometime in the 1880s. It continued operating until the mid-1890's."

The earliest flour mill was constructed of wood sometime between 1854 and 1857 in what is now west Silver Lake Park between 7th and 9th Street NE (maps vary), north of the former fire station. Initially called the Zumbro Falls Mills, it was acquired by John M. Cole between 1857 and 1860 through a bankruptcy proceeding, after which it was known as Cole's Mill or the Lower Town Mill. It was powered by a millrace running from a millpond on the site of the Silver Lake Power Plant. A dam across the Zumbro just south of Silver Creek maintained the water level in the pond. Cole made many improvements to the mill and was highly regarded as a businessman.

Flour suspended in air is explosive, and flour mills are notoriously fire prone. Cole's Mill was destroyed by fire in 1878 and rebuilt the following year by Cole. On August 21, 1883, a tornado damaged the mill badly, tearing off the roof and the west end of the building, destroying machinery and outbuildings and scattering railroad cars like toys. Worse yet, Cole was killed by the storm. His body was found in the street between the mill and his residence. The mill was taken over by Cole's son, John A., and repaired. In 1890, it burned to the ground and was replaced again. It was in operation until 1910. Its fate in later years is not recorded. At some point, the city acquired the property, and in 1931 the city council voted to demolish the mill and fill in the shallow remains of the millpond, where the Silver Lake power plant was built in 1947.

The other early flour mill was built in 1856–57 on the west bank of the Zumbro at the foot of 3rd Street by Frederick A. Olds, often called "Judge Olds." It was a stone structure, forty-six by seventy feet with five-foot-thick walls. Stone for the walls was quarried locally and hauled by oxen teams. The beams and floor were hand-hewn oak from the virgin forests near Genoa. The mill was powered by a millrace that started at a bend in the river at what is now 1st Avenue and 6th Street SW. It ran north and east in a straight line, running under Broadway and what is now the Riverside Building and the alley behind businesses on the East 300 block of South Broadway. Olds was joined by his son-in-law, Thomas L. Fishback, in 1857, after which the mill was called the Olds and Fishback Mill. Judge Olds served as mayor of Rochester in 1859–60. He died at the age of fifty-four in 1864 after a fall from the roof of his barn. After that, his son,

Cole's Mill after 1883 tornado. *Courtesy of the History Center of Olmsted County.*

Frederick T. Olds, partnered with Fishback in running the mill. The mill was beautifully depicted in a woodblock engraving in the 1874 Andreas' *Illustrated Historical Atlas of the State of Minnesota.*[12] In the days before fire hydrants were installed, the Olds and Fishback millrace was also used to provide water for the fire department via a steam-driven pump positioned just south of the mill. In 1883, Fishback sold out to F.T. Olds, who then sold out to John A. Cole, owner of the Zumbro Mill. Thereafter, the two mills were operated in tandem as John A. Cole Milling Company, leading to some confusion regarding the use of the name "Cole's Mill." The mill was improved by changing from the original "burr" mill to a roller mill and addition of a one-hundred-horsepower engine to back up the waterpower. By 1910, the mill was said to be capable of milling 1,000 bushels of wheat into 250 barrels of flour per day. It was used to grind high-grade flour, while the other Cole's/Zumbro/Lower Town mill was used to grind feed and coarse grain (rye and buckwheat). In 1910, the company was renamed Rochester Milling Co., and in 1912, William Knapp bought out Cole but died September 16 of the same year at age fifty-eight. His sons, Spencer and Harold,[13] ran the mill until the late 1920s. The milling business waned as wheat growers in Minnesota transitioned to other crops; 80 percent of flour mills in Minnesota closed in the 1920s. The mill was abandoned for a few years and then taken over by the city in the early 1930s. It was a local landmark, the "Old Stone Mill." Part of it was rented out as a farm service store; other parts were rented to businesses for storage until 1951, when part of the building was demolished, followed by the remainder in 1953. The millrace was covered over, and segments were removed piecemeal as construction took place along its course. The mill reservation (south of the mill bordering on 4th Street) was purchased on September 26, 1930, by Mayo Properties Association. They added a retaining wall along the west bank of the Zumbro north of 4th Street, built an alley behind Broadway businesses and filled the land up to street level, covering over the millrace. On the two properties created between the alley and the river, a Red Owl grocery was built in 1935 or 1936. The Time Theater was built in 1936 to 1937.

Cascade Mill, also called Tondro's Mill or Thompson's Mill, was built in 1864 by John S. Humason and Gilbert Smith. It was at the end of Cascade Creek just before it joins the Zumbro west of North Broadway in what is now called Thompson Mill Race Park. In 1867, Humason sold it to Lewis and Abraham Harkins, who improved it, then sold it to Lyman Tondro in 1871. Between 1877 and 1879, Tondro added a steam engine to the mill. The boiler was housed in an outbuilding, the stone walls of which are all that remains of the mill. The mill was damaged by the 1883 tornado but repaired by Tondro. Because of declining health, he sold the mill to Clarence Thompson in 1903. Thompson's family owned it until 1986, when they donated it to the city as a park.

A steam-powered flour mill was built on the west side of Broadway south of College Street (4th Street S) in 1874 by J.B. Bassett and L.T. Hulbert. It was substantial with six "runs of stone" but apparently was not profitable. It was abandoned after 1880 and destroyed by a fire in 1889. Other mills in the city included the Broadway Roller Mills of Buttles and Herrick, at Broadway and 7th Street (2nd Street North) started in 1871, initially a furniture and lumber planing mill, later a flouring mill, dissolved in 1887. The Queen City Feed Mill operated at Broadway and 6th Street (1st Street NW) briefly in 1900–1901.

The second woolen mill, called Rochester Woolen Mills, was built by C.T. Booth in 1896–97 next to Cole's Zumbro Mill. The building was wooden, 74 by 50 feet and three stories high. The opening of the mill was delayed by a fire that necessitated extensive reconstruction. The first three years of operation were promising. The initial product was high-quality blankets. In 1899, Booth moved to Georgia, and Henry K. Terry, a businessman from Connecticut, assumed management of the business, changing the product to woolen clothing rather than blankets. In 1900, Terry recruited local investors to build a brick factory (now called the Conley-Maass Building) on College (4th) Street near Broadway for manufacturing wool pants. Initial popularity did not last, and by 1903 finances were disappointing and the business closed, leaving the factory building to be taken over by Conley Cameras (see pages 60–64). In 1904, the mill machinery was sold to a woolen mill in Braden, Oregon, and the mill building was demolished in 1909.

Each of the Rochester and Olmsted mills had less than twenty feet of waterfall to power it. Outside of Rochester, the historically notable mills of Olmsted County included Fugle's Mill, Stewart's Mill, Allis's Mill, Genoa's sawmills and Potsdam's windmill.

Oronoco has greater waterpower than Rochester with four branches of the Zumbro converging there. The first mill in Oronoco was built by George W. Wirt but named after Abraham D. Allis, who bought it in 1863 and improved it. He enlarged it further in 1873 with eight millstones, but it burned in 1889 and was rebuilt on a smaller scale. Its millpond was called Lake Allis, later renamed Lake Shady. It was the summer recreation hot spot for the well-to-do of Rochester until Lake Zumbro was created in 1919. The fortunate few included the Drs. Will and Charlie Mayo, who shared a summer cottage on its northeast shore, later owned by Harry Harwick, who built a substantial Ellerbe-designed house on the lot. The Rochester State Hospital also had a facility on the south side of the lake to provide summertime recreation for its patients.

Matthew Fugh built a gristmill in Pleasant Grove Township in 1871. The building still stands along the North Branch of the Root River off County

Lake Shady (Lake Allis) with Allis's Mill on left, Horton's first bridge in background. *Postcard image.*

Road 1, two miles south of Simpson. It was once a tourist attraction but is now privately owned and not open to the public. I have not seen an explanation of the slight name change to Fugle's Mill, which Leonard did not mention in his 1910 history. Perhaps it was anglicized along with many other German names during and after World War I.

Stewart's Mill was a flour mill built in 1857 by Charles Stewart on the North Branch of the Root River three miles east of High Forest. It was the commercial nucleus that prompted the growth of Stewartville. Its dam created a lake that was called Lake Alice until at least 1910 in honor of Stewart's wife. But by 1916, it was known as Lake Florence after his daughter-in-law, possibly because of confusion with Lake Allis (Shady) in Oronoco. It was reported that Florence Stewart lost a diamond ring while dangling her hand over the side of a boat. It was never found. Lake Florence was a regional recreational center for Stewartville for over a century until 1993, when the dam collapsed during the spring snowmelt and was never rebuilt. Florence Park now lies in the bed of Lake Florence. Remnants of the dam can still be seen along the banks of the Root River.

New Haven and Kalmar Townships were home to the Big Woods of Olmsted County, so sawmills were needed to produce lumber for construction and furniture production in Rochester and Olmsted County. The first was built in Durango (later renamed New Haven) in 1857. That

BAETON & CORINSKY _ POTSDAM FLOURING MILL, FARMINGTON TP.
OLMSTED CO.

Potsdam
Flouring Mill.
From Andreas's
Historical Atlas
of the State
of Minnesota,
1874.

closed after a dam washout in 1864. A series of water-driven and steam-driven sawmills were built in Genoa through the 1850s and 1860s. Lumber production eventually faded as the supply of old-growth trees was exhausted and cheaper pine lumber was brought by the railroads.

Near Potsdam, Baeton & Corinsky's wind-driven flour mill was built in 1874 as a cooperative venture of local farmers. It cast a striking image on high ground, visible for miles around. The following April, a strong wind blew the mill out of control. Four young men climbed the tower to attempt to control it. One was knocked down into the mechanism and was literally "run through the mill" and crushed. A less grisly but similarly fatal wind-driven incident occurred in December 1876. The wind-driven mechanism was replaced by a gasoline engine, making it safer.

A less gruesome but more commonly lethal mill-related hazard was drowning in the millponds. Leonard described the drowning of nine people, mostly children, in about thirty years in Lake Allis (Shady) alone.[14]

WALTER LOWRY BRACKENRIDGE, 1855

Walter Lowry Brackenridge was born in Butler County, near Meadville, Pennsylvania, on November 5, 1824. He studied law and was admitted to the bar in Pennsylvania in 1853. He visited Olmsted County in 1855 and moved to Rochester the following year with his wife, Margaret Logan, who later recalled that there were two stores on Broadway and two log cabins east of the river when they first arrived. As an attorney, Walter was renowned for the strength and success of his oral arguments, particularly regarding pending legislation. Naturally, real estate in the new town was a large part of his legal practice. He saw great value in real estate and acquired enormous tracts (over one thousand acres) of farmland, mainly in Marion Township, as well as numerous commercial properties in town. His practice was general law until the Winona and St. Peter Railroad came to town in 1863, after which he served as attorney for the company for twelve years. His health forced him to retire in 1876. He spent his remaining years managing his extensive real estate holdings. (In 1896, he owned 1,110 acres [1.73 square miles] in five parcels in Marion Township, plus 80 acres in Viola Township, 14 acres in Pleasant Grove Township and 33 acres adjacent to his house in southeast Rochester.) He died of Bright's disease (kidney failure) on August 29, 1899, at the age of seventy-four. Margaret died in October 1914. Among her pallbearers were both Mayo brothers, Burt Eaton, David Berkman and A.C. Gooding. The Brackenridge family plot in Oakwood Cemetery is marked by an enormous obelisk and sits adjacent to the Mayo family plot and the Van Dusen mausoleum.

Walter and Margaret had three children: Logan, Madge and Blanche. Their son William L. (Logan) also became a prominent Rochester attorney. After graduating from the law school of the University of Michigan in 1879, he joined the firm of Start and Gove. After 1884, he was in solo practice. He served as city attorney for six years and county attorney for four years and was renowned as a prosecutor. In 1905, he died of respiratory complications after otherwise successful surgery for symptomatic gallstones. He was unmarried and only forty-eight years of age. Logan's two sisters were Margaret (Madge), who married hardware retailer G.D. Parmele, and Elizabeth (Blanche), who married Dr. Christopher Graham.

The first Brackenridge house was built in 1856 at the northwest corner of 5th (Center) Street and Main Street (1st Avenue W.). It was described by Leonard as "at that time noticeable as probably the best home in the town." Their second was built in 1865 on the lot just north of the first. Walter

Right: Walter Lowry Brackenridge. *From Hon. Joseph A. Leonard,* History of Olmsted County Minnesota, *1910.*

Below: Brackenridge house. *Courtesy of the History Center of Olmsted County.*

Opposite: Graham house. *Courtesy of the History Center of Olmsted County.*

used the first house for his law office. Both were eventually replaced by the Colonial Hotel/Hospital. They bought their magnificent third house and thirty-three acres of farmland at 813 Dubuque Street (3rd Avenue SE) in 1872 from William Dundas Lowry, a relative. After Walter died, Logan lived in the house with his mother, Margaret. When Logan died in 1905, the house was passed to Blanche and her husband, Dr. Christopher Graham. After Margaret died in 1914, they remodeled the house extensively in 1917–19. Harold Crawford designed the transformation from Victorian style to Georgian style. Thereafter, it was known as the Graham Estate. It was a local landmark for many years. Dr. Graham died in 1952 and Blanche died in 1961, after which their son Malcolm lived in the house until his death in 1964. The house sat mostly empty until Malcolm's sister Elizabeth sold the house and grounds in 1970, at which point it was demolished to make way for a Kmart.[15]

In addition to the Brackenridge properties, inherited by Blanche and her sister Madge, Christopher Graham owned tremendous land holdings, acquired both by inheritance and from his own investments. In 1914, he owned 2,646 acres (4.13 square miles) in Kalmar, Cascade, Rochester and Salem Townships.[16] When he left the Mayo partnership and the practice of medicine in 1919, he remained busy and wealthy.

Captain Dan Heaney, 1855

Daniel D. Heaney was born in 1831 on the Isle of Man, the son of an Irish father and Scottish mother. He came to Rochester in 1855 from Indiana and worked for John R. Cook (who founded the First National Bank and built the Cook Hotel). In 1857, he owned a store and mill in Durango. In June 1861, Company B of the Second Minnesota Regiment was formed, led by Captain William Markham, First Lieutenant Daniel Heaney and Second Lieutenant Abram Harkins. Heaney was promoted to captain of Company C on December 4, 1861. The Second Regiment distinguished themselves in the Union victory at Mill Springs and repulsed the rebels at Chickamauga. Heaney later served as adjutant to Colonel Horatio P. Van Cleve (Second Minnesota Regiment) and still later as quartermaster for the Army of Cumberland and Ohio until the end of the Civil War. Before he left to serve in the war, Heaney purchased the empty lot on the northwest corner of Broadway and Zumbro Street (2nd Street South).

After the war, he returned to Rochester, apparently much wealthier, and resumed business along with breeding of racehorses using premium stock he brought from Kentucky. Rochester was noted for fine and fast horses for many years after. Heaney was instrumental in establishing the original county fairgrounds (at what is now Soldiers Field) and its racetrack to the southeast. The pride of his stable was a stallion named Star of the West, which he bought in 1868 for $5,000. The source of his wealth is not stated; however, in 1866, of the eighty-six Rochester residents with the highest declared incomes, Heaney's was second, more than three times the average of the highest rollers.[17]

In 1866–67, Heaney, in partnership with his uncle George Moon, funded the construction of the Heaney Block. It was designed by architect W.W. Boyington of Chicago and built by Granville Woodworth at the northwest corner of Zumbro Street and Broadway. Built with the finest materials, at 110 by 100 feet, it was the largest and best commercial building in Rochester at the time. Above a full basement with billiard hall, it had three more levels. On the ground level was First National Bank and five stores. Offices for prominent professionals (including C.C. Willson and, briefly, W.W. Mayo) filled the second floor, and the top level was Heaney's Opera House, Rochester's principal theater until the Metropolitan opened in 1902. It was fully rented when it opened and remained the premier business address in the city.

In 1868, Heaney owned 469 acres of farmland in Cascade, New Haven and Rochester Townships, much of it near the north and west edges of town.

He served as the ninth mayor of Rochester in 1869–70. Joseph A. Leonard said of him: "He was liberal and generous and exceedingly popular."

Trouble was suggested when Heaney's partnership with John J. Cooke was dissolved in December 1869 and when his partnership with Peter F. Lawshe was dissolved in April 1871. In each case, Heaney assumed the liabilities and his former partner received the assets of the dissolved firm. In July 1876, Heaney's career skidded to a halt as the *Rochester Post* announced: "Capt. D. Heaney was adjudged insane and sent to St. Peter, on Friday of last week." The following year his wife, Mattie, was granted divorce and custody of their two young children, Will and Mattie, based on his "intemperance, adultery and improvident use of property." On October 21, 1876, the *Rochester Post* noted the sale of the Heaney Block to J.D. Blake, F.T. Olds, T.L. Fishback and H.E. Horton for less than half of the original cost of construction. It noted: "It is fortunate that this valuable property has fallen into the hands of these reliable and enterprising men." The Heaney Block was thereafter called the Horton Block, and Heaney's Opera House was renamed the Grand Opera House. Sales of the Heaney farms and the Heaney residential property followed. With his name effaced, Heaney was mostly forgotten.

Star of the West was sold and died in 1891 in Muscatine, Iowa, at the age of thirty-two after a prolific racing and stud career. Mattie Heaney (Dan's ex-wife) died in Kentucky in 1904. Captain Heaney lived out his later years as a resident of the Minnesota Soldier's Home in Minneapolis. He died in Hennepin County on February 6, 1918. He was cremated, and his ashes were interred in Spokane, Washington (where his daughter lived).

On January 11, 1917, fifty years and a day after it opened, the Heaney/Horton Block and all of its eighteen businesses were consumed by the greatest fire in Rochester history to that date. It was replaced by E.A. Knowlton & Co. department store, which, in turn, was replaced by Dayton's in 1954 (since renamed Rosa Parks Pavilion by Mayo Clinic).[18]

NICHOLAS BREWER, 1857

Nicholas Richard Brewer (1857–1949) was a portrait and landscape painter of renown in the late nineteenth and early twentieth centuries.[19] He was born and raised on a pioneer farm a mile west of High Forest, on the North Branch of the Root River, fifteen miles southwest of Rochester. He was born the year before High Forest Township and Rochester were incorporated. He had limited formal education and was mainly self-taught as an artist. He also learned his trade partly from a series of mentors, including D.W. Tryon and Charles Noel Flagg. Subjects of his portraits included many politicians and tycoons throughout the country, including Minnesota railroad magnate James J. Hill, St. Paul archbishop John Ireland, many actors, musicians and socialites as well as governors, senators, congressmen, judges and U.S. presidents Ulysses S. Grant and Franklin Delano Roosevelt. He traveled extensively, showing and lecturing about his work. He lived mainly in St. Paul but also in New York and Chicago and for a period in Arkansas.

Brewer's autobiography, *Trails of a Paintbrush*, was published in 1938 and republished in 2021. He depicts his life growing up in pioneer days in rural Minnesota, with earliest recollections before and during the Dakota War of 1862. He describes a peaceful but tense encounter with Marpiya Okinajin (a member of the Mdewakanton Tribe, known among English speakers as "Cut-Nose," who was among the thirty-eight executed in Mankato in 1862). Brewer was proud of making a living as an artist; in fact, his first earnings came from raffling off his art when he was eight years old. He migrated to St. Paul and later New York, at times barely eking out an existence but sustaining his art. With some difficulty, particularly early in his career, he was able to provide for his wife and six sons (four of whom became artists). He was progressively more renowned later in life, although his art, both portraits and landscapes, lost popularity late in his life as photography replaced much of his former demand. The book includes his commentary on the evolving art world, particularly his dislike for abstract art in the late nineteenth and early twentieth centuries. Overall, the book is a good resource for anyone contemplating the life of an artist, particularly when "thinking of quitting one's day-job." A recent biography, by Julie L'Enfant, explores more of his social context and family legacy and is richly illustrated with his works.[20]

Brewer's works are in the collections of the Art Institute of Chicago; the National Gallery in Washington, D.C.; the High Museum in Atlanta; the Arkansas Museum of Fine Arts; the Butler Institute of American Art in Youngstown, Ohio; the Weisman Art Museum in Minneapolis; the Minneapolis Institute of Arts; and the Minnesota Historical Society, among others. His works have been exhibited by the Minnesota Historical Society, the Minnesota State Art Society, the Minneapolis Institute of Art, Museum of Fine Arts in Houston and Carnegie Institute in Pittsburgh.

C.C. Willson and Willson's Castle, 1858

Charles Cudworth Willson (known as C.C.) was born in Cattaraugus County, New York, just south of Buffalo, on October 27, 1829. He studied law and was admitted to the bar in Genesee County, New York, in 1851. He visited Rochester, Minnesota, in 1856, then settled here in 1858 and established his legal practice. He married Annie K. Rosebrugh in 1862. They had nine children.

Willson was highly respected in his legal practice, with offices in the Heaney Block, the premier offices in the city. He was the most senior member of the bar of Olmsted County. He practiced for sixty-two years in Rochester. He never had a partner but mentored a number of junior associates, including Frank Kellogg, Burt Eaton and Charles Start. He did not engage in politics except for a single term on the school board. In 1892, he was appointed the official reporter of the proceedings of the Minnesota Supreme Court, a role in which he served for four years.

Like some other early settlers, Willson had landholdings that contributed to his wealth. He owned a 1,480-acre grain farm in Haverhill Township near the current site of Century High School. For comparison, the Century campus is 105 acres.

In 1860, after George Head had acquired most of the land on College Hill (4th Street SW), Willson purchased from Head a two-square-block tract at the top of the hill bordered by College and 1st Streets (4th and 6th Streets SW) and State and Cutler Street (9th and 10th Avenues SW). He built a mansion with thirty-two rooms (after 1878 addition), the largest house in Rochester at the time, at the southwest corner of College and State Streets, the highest point in town. It was built of red brick on a limestone foundation with white trim. Interior woodwork was clear black walnut, likely from the virgin forests near Genoa. He called the distinctive house Red Oaks, but it was quickly nicknamed "Willson's Castle." The original portion of the house, the two-story northern wing, was completed in 1864. In 1878, he more than doubled the size of the house by adding the more ornate south wing (which projected to the east) and the three-story, seventy-five-foot-tall tower at the intersection of the two wings.

Annie died in 1911. Early in 1918, at the age of eighty-nine, Willson moved into the College Apartments, four blocks down College Hill, with one of his daughters. The Castle sat empty for a few months until a hot, dry day in the summer when lightning caused a grass fire that spread to the house. The Rochester Fire Department responded quickly but found to their

RESIDENCE OF C.C.WILLSON
ROCHESTER MINN. 2.06.

Red Oaks or "Willson's Castle." *Postcard image.*

C.C. Willson's grave. *Photo by Paul David Scanlon.*

chagrin that the standpipe water tank in St. Mary's Park across the street did not have enough pressure to drive their hoses. The house had its own water supply pumped to a storage tank in the tower. Before the firefighters could access it, it crashed to the ground as the tower burned. The firefighters watched helplessly as the house was consumed by fire. Ironically, there had been a fire on Willson's property in 1901 in which a fire was contained to an attached woodshed. The same water pressure problem occurred then, but control was achieved with two "chemical engines" plus hand-carried water.[21] The necessary improvements in the standpipe at St. Mary's Park were made in 1922, too late for Willson's Castle.

Willson died on November 1, 1922. He is buried beside his wife and several children with a massive grave marker in Oakwood Cemetery north of the Healy Chapel. Several years after Willson's death, the ruins of the house were buried in the remains of the foundation and covered with soil and landscaping. When I was a child, the remnants of the foundation could still be seen at the southwest corner of the lot.[22]

COLONEL GEORGE HEALY
AND OAKWOOD CEMETERY, 1859

George Healy was born on August 19, 1812, in Cayuga County, New York. He grew up on a farm but was trained as a civil engineer and surveyor. He worked as a civil engineer for the Erie Canal and the New York and Erie Railroads. On October 6, 1841, he married Theodosia Polhemus. At about that time, he served in the 213th Regiment of the New York militia as colonel. He moved to Rochester in the spring of 1859 at the age of forty-six. In 1860, he introduced high-quality Merino sheep to farmers in the region. He worked as a civil engineer and was surveyor for both Rochester and Olmsted County. His greatest source of wealth was as a moneylender. At different times, he owned twenty-one farms in Minnesota and, between 1868 and 1896, a total of 428 acres in Olmsted County. He also developed extensive tracts of residential real estate.

Healy was an amateur meteorologist who kept scrupulously detailed and accurate and now valued records of the weather in the pioneer period. He built the first brick residence in the city at the corner of Franklin (2nd Avenue SW) and 3rd Streets. It had a tower from which he made measurements of the weather and the correct time. George and Theodosia had two children. George P. died as an infant in 1946, and Mary Amie died at the age of thirteen. An adopted daughter, Dolly, lived to adulthood but never married.

He was the inaugural president of the Rochester Cemetery Association from 1862 to 1876 and did the original survey and design of Oakwood Cemetery in 1863. In 1889–90, he funded the construction of the Healy Vault for wintertime storage of bodies when the ground was frozen. The initial vault had a capacity for twenty-five caskets and was near the entrance to the cemetery.

In 1895, Healy pledged $5,000 to the public library for the purchase of books, insisting that it include books with liberal religious and political ideas. With great controversy, the library board approved acceptance of the gift by a single vote majority, with a tie-breaking vote by library board president Burt Eaton.

Healy died the following year, August 11, 1896, leaving 70 percent of his estate to the Oakwood Cemetery Association. Theodosia had died in 1882 and Dolly the previous year. They are all buried in Oakwood Cemetery in graves marked by an unusual monument in the shape of a sextant, which he used for some of his astronomical calculations. Around the perimeter of his grave site, he had stone replicas of log cabin foundation logs placed

Healy grave marker. *Photo by Paul David Scanlon.*

to "stake his claim." Some of his bequest was used in 1912 to construct the Healy Memorial Chapel in Oakwood. It was built with Bedford stone by Garfield Schwartz & Co. A newer and larger vault was built under the chapel, accessible from the rear. Curiously, the engraved stone lintel of the 1890 vault was placed over the newer vault.

Left: Healy vault. *Photo by Paul David Scanlon.*

Below: Healy Chapel. *Postcard image.*

The beautiful arched entrance to Oakwood Cemetery was designed by Ray Corwin of the Ellerbe firm, who also designed the decorative elements of both the Plummer Building and the Chateau Theater. Funding for the archway was provided in 1927 and 1928 as a tribute to early Rochester builder Granville Woodworth by his daughters Mary and Flora. A large, embellished map of all the burial plots in Oakwood was created by Harold Crawford.[23]

BIRTH OF THE MINNESOTA EDUCATION ASSOCIATION, 1861

The following text is from a memorial plaque in Mayo Park:

"August 27, 1961, marked the centennial observance of the founding of the [Minnesota Education Association] MEA. This organization, with its more than 28,000 classroom teachers and administrators and with its headquarters in St. Paul, was formed at Rochester during the early days of the Civil War. John Ogden, principal of the First State Normal at Winona and Jabez Brooks, later president of Hamline University at Red Wing, hoped that through organization the teaching profession might advance the cause of the common school and thus better serve the needs of the new state.

"Meeting in the little Baptist Church at the bend of the Zumbro River west of the Mayo Park bridge, some 50 pioneer teachers of Minnesota dedicated themselves 'to elevate the character and advance the interests of the teaching profession and to promote the cause of popular education.' Benjamin F. Crary, state superintendent of public instruction, St. Paul, was elected president of the association at this first meeting; A.D. Williams, president (principal), Wasioja Seminary, vice president; S.T. Jones, village schoolmaster, Mantorville, secretary; and O.O. Baldwin, superintendent, Rochester, treasurer.

"From the past of each of us come enduring memories of a classroom teacher who took our hand and helped to make of our lives something better than it might otherwise have been. To their memory this marker is dedicated."

JUDGE CHARLES START, 1863

Charles Monroe Start was born on October 4, 1839, in Bakersfield, Vermont, near the Canadian border, the son of a farmer who also served as justice of the peace for twenty-five years. Start attended local schools and the nearby Barre Academy, then studied law with Judge William C. Wilson of Bakersfield until July 1862, when he enlisted as a private in the Tenth Vermont Volunteer Regiment. After a short while, he was commissioned as a lieutenant for the Civil War. While stationed west of Washington, D.C., awaiting deployment, Start and many of his regiment became ill. In December 1862, he resigned his commission and returned to Vermont to recover his health. The following October 1863, he moved to Rochester, Minnesota, and interned in the law office of C.C. Willson. In 1864, he was elected Rochester city attorney.

On August 10, 1865, Start married Clara Wilson, the daughter of his Vermont mentor, in Bakersfield. They lived in Rochester on the southwest corner of College and Glencoe Streets (4th Street and 6th Avenue SW where High Point Condominium is now). Their first child, a daughter named Lizzie, died in infancy in 1866. A second daughter, Clara, was born in 1869.

In 1871, Start was elected county attorney for Olmsted County. He served eight years until 1879, when he was elected attorney general of Minnesota. In 1881, he was appointed judge of the Third Judicial District by Governor John Pillsbury. Start was reelected twice without opposition. In 1895, he was

Chas. M. Start

Judge Charles Start. *Courtesy of the History Center of Olmsted County.*

elected chief justice of the Minnesota Supreme Court, the first from Rochester to serve in that role. Known as a guardian of individual rights and liberties, he wrote more than one thousand opinions during his years on the Supreme Court. He was reelected unopposed twice and served until his retirement in 1913 at the age of seventy-three. Start's younger brother, Henry, served as a member of the Vermont Supreme Court.

Judge Start died at the age of eighty on December 19, 1919, in St. Paul. He was beloved and respected by colleagues and the populace. Memorial services were held in both St. Paul and Rochester. Many of his colleagues spoke in his tribute, including the Honorable Thomas S. Buckham, who said: "He was a man who in his every action showed a strong, genuine sympathy with what has come to be called the average man." The Honorable Frank B. Kellogg said: "He was liberal in his political views. The champion of the weak and unfortunate, with an unshakeable confidence in the wisdom of democratic institutions and in the destiny of his country."[24] Charles Start is buried in Oakwood Cemetery beside his wife, Clara, who died in 1924.[25]

MEDAL OF HONOR RECIPIENTS OF OLMSTED COUNTY, 1864

Alonzo Pickle was born in 1843 in Quebec. In 1857, his family moved to a farm between Dover and Eyota. In August 1862, he joined Company B, First Battalion Minnesota Infantry, in St. Charles. In four years of Civil War duty, he participated in twelve major battles, including First and Second Fredericksburg, Bristoe Station and Gettysburg. He was one of the few who survived the heroic and crucial charge of the First Minnesota Regiment at Gettysburg. President Coolidge described them as "the saviors of their country." Pickle was awarded the Medal of Honor on June 12, 1895, for gallantry at Deep Bottom, Virginia, where on August 14, 1864, "at the risk of his life, [he]voluntarily went to the assistance of a wounded officer lying close to the enemy's lines and, under fire, carried him to a place of safety." Pickle was present when General Robert E. Lee surrendered at Appomattox, Virginia. After the war, he settled in Sleepy Eye, Minnesota, where he died on May 24, 1925, and was buried.

Two names are paired. Both enrolled in Rochester, but neither was a Rochester resident. John Vale (b. August 9, 1836, borough of Lambeth, London, England) arrived in New York on November 12, 1851, farmed in Blue Earth County, Minnesota Territory, and enlisted in Rochester on July 15, 1861. Byron Edward Pay (b. October 21, 1844, Le Ray Township, Jefferson County, New York) worked on his brother's farm in Blue Earth County and enlisted in Rochester on June 22, 1861, at age sixteen. Both were inducted in Rochester as privates into Company H, Second Minnesota Regiment. At Nolensville, Tennessee, on February 15, 1863, each "was one of a detachment of 16 men who heroically defended a wagon train against the attack of 125 cavalry, repulsed the attack and saved the train." Pay was discharged after the Battle of Chickamauga, where he suffered a gunshot wound to the shoulder. Vale served the entire war with distinction in many battles. He was never injured and attained the rank of sergeant. On September 11, 1897, Vale and Pay were among eight surviving members of Company H who were awarded the Medal of Honor. After the war, Vale settled briefly in Rochester before moving to Davenport, Iowa, where he died on February 4, 1909, and was buried. Pay died on February 19, 1906, in Volga, South Dakota, and is buried in Arlington National Cemetery.

John Johnson was born on March 25, 1842, in Oslo, Norway. He enlisted in the Second Wisconsin Infantry in Janesville, Wisconsin, and fought in the Battles of Antietam and Fredericksburg. On December 13, 1862, at Fredericksburg, Johnson was in a gunnery crew and lost his right arm to shrapnel. He continued to load cannons until he passed out from blood loss. After the war, he farmed in Salem Township in the 1880s and perhaps later. He was awarded the Medal of Honor on August 28, 1893, for "conspicuous gallantry in battle in which he was severely wounded." He died on April 3, 1907, in Washington, D.C., and is buried in Rock Creek Cemetery.[26]

THE HEFFRON BROTHERS, 1864

Christopher H. Heffron was born in Maine on Christmas 1852, the eldest of four sons of Patrick and Margaret (O'Brien) Heffron, both Irish Catholic immigrants. The young family moved to New York City, where Martin Francis was born on April 2, 1953, and Patrick Richard on June 1, 1856. The last brother, John, was born in Wisconsin on February 22, 1861. Little is known of John other than his death in Rochester on December 12, 1913. The family moved to Rochester in 1864 and to a farm in Kalmar Township in 1865. The father worked as a carpenter and became a successful contractor, primarily building houses. The boys grew up on the family farm with a country school education but access to books from their parents, who were both well-read.

Christopher taught in county schools for several years and then was appointed deputy clerk of Olmsted County court, a role in which he served four years. He was then elected clerk of court and served with distinction for thirteen years. He then became a clerk in the United States review office in St. Paul. He died in 1924 at the age of seventy-one and is buried in Calvary Cemetery.

Martin passed the teaching exam at a young age and taught school for nine years. From 1880 to 1886, he worked as deputy clerk of court for his older brother Christopher, the clerk of court. Meanwhile, he learned building from his father. Beginning in 1881, he built houses, then larger projects, leaving his court position in 1886. He made the initial modifications for, and addition to, St. Mary's Hall at the Academy of Our Lady of Lourdes in 1882 (see pages 52–57). He built parts of the Schuster Brewery, parts of the Rochester State Hospital, the first major addition to the Academy of Our Lady of Lourdes (1888) and the original St. Mary's Hospital building, completed in 1889.

In 1889, at the age of forty-one, he began working for Charles W. Gindele Co. of Chicago, building large government and commercial projects for four or five years. He then returned to Rochester and resumed his construction business, taking on larger projects. He built all of the additions to St. Mary's Hospital from the first in 1893 to the final expansion of the chapel in 1931, the Conley-Maass Building in 1900, a remodeling of and addition to St. Mary's Hall at the Academy of Our Lady of Lourdes in 1900, the Metropolitan Opera House, the Young Men's Christian Association building on Zumbro Street (2nd Street SW) and the second major addition to the Academy of Our Lady of Lourdes in 1908. St. John's Parish hired him for a 1900 addition to and remodeling of the 1872 church, then for a rectory in 1909 and Heffron High School for boys (named for Heffron's brother Patrick, who was the second bishop of the Diocese of Winona), plus St. John's Parochial School (elementary on first floor, girls' high school on the second floor), all in 1913.

He completed St. Teresa Hall and St. Cecilia Hall at the College of St. Teresa in Winona in 1912, both designed by Erhard Brielmaier.

Martin married Margaret McElligott in 1899. They had one son, Maurice, and an adopted daughter, Luella. He was elected alderman for two terms (1899–1903) and served as mayor of Rochester in 1905–7. From 1910 to 1938, he served on the board of Olmsted County Savings and Loan.

In 1920, at age sixty-two, Martin partnered with thirty-two-year-old Rochester native William Fitzgerald, who had worked for Heffron as a bookkeeper in 1908. Fitzgerald learned commercial contracting during ten years with Garfield Schwartz & Co., during which he served as construction supervisor for Mayo Clinic's 1914 red brick building. Together as Heffron & Fitzgerald Construction Co., they remodeled and added to St. Mary's Hall in 1921, built the 1922 surgical building for St. Mary's Hospital (later called the Joseph Building), four more new buildings at the College of St. Teresa in Winona,[27] the Chateau Theater (in 1927 in only seven months!), several later additions to St. Mary's Hospital, as well as many churches, residences and commercial buildings in the region. In 1933, the Depression brought an end to the building boom, and Heffron & Fitzgerald closed shop. Heffron's wife died in 1936. In July 1938, he traveled to Dickinson, North Dakota, to visit his son, Dr. Maurice Heffron. His health deteriorated, and he died on September 15 at the age of eighty-five. William Fitzgerald died in 1939, the same year as the Mayo brothers and Sister Joseph. Both Martin Heffron and William Fitzgerald are buried in Calvary Cemetery in Rochester.[28]

Patrick Richard Heffron was born in New York in 1860, two years younger than his brother Martin. He was ordained as a Catholic priest in St. Paul in 1884. In 1910, he was appointed the second bishop of the Diocese of Winona (after Bishop Joseph Bernard Cotter). He served until his death from cancer on November 23, 1927. He is buried in St. Mary's Cemetery in Winona. He is considered the founder of St. Mary's College (now St. Mary's University or SMU) in Winona as well as Cotter High School in Winona and Heffron High School in Rochester. Heffron Hall, an historic residence hall for upper-class students at SMU, is named in his honor. On August 27, 1915, a disturbed priest named Laurence M. Lesches shot Bishop Heffron twice while he was celebrating mass. The bishop survived, and Lesches was committed to the insane asylum in St. Peter, where he remained for the rest of his life, dying in 1943. It is rumored that Heffron Hall is haunted by the ghost of Lesches.[29]

GEORGE W. VAN DUSEN, 1865

The largest and most elegant mausoleum in Oakwood Cemetery has "G.W. Van Dusen" inscribed on the lintel. Who was this? George Washington Van Dusen was born near Rochester, New York, on July 10, 1826. In 1849, he moved to Wisconsin, where he worked as a farmer and grain buyer. He moved to Rochester, Minnesota, in 1864, the year after the Winona and St. Peter Railroad line extended to Rochester. He was a partner for five years in the dry goods firm of Barden, Baldwin & Van Dusen. He worked briefly for the Chicago and Northwestern Railroad as a grain buyer, then formed a grain buying partnership with C.H. Chadbourn. Beginning in 1865, he built warehouses and grain elevators along the

George Van Dusen. *Courtesy of the History Center of Olmsted County.*

Winona and St. Peter Line (taken over by the Chicago and Northwestern in 1867) as G.W. Van Dusen & Co. In 1869, together with Thomas J. Templar, he built an elevator and warehouse ten miles west of Rochester near a village called Bear Grove. Van Dusen platted a new village slightly east of Bear Grove and is credited with renaming it Byron as a tribute to his father's birthplace, Byron Center, in Genesee County, New York, as well as the town of Port Byron, New York, where George had once lived.

The elevator and grain trade business was enormously profitable for Van Dusen. He was also very civic minded and served on the city council as alderman and served one term as mayor from 1872 to 1873. His stately Rochester homestead is depicted in a woodcut illustration of Andreas's 1874 *Atlas of the State of Minnesota.* Because of his grain business, he eventually moved to Minneapolis, though he maintained relationships in Rochester and continued to spend time with friends and associates here.

By 1888, Van Dusen's company controlled more than ninety elevators as far west as Pierre, South Dakota. He was also president and general manager of the Star Elevator Company. That year, the two companies were merged in a sale to British investors. The company reemerged the following year as Van Dusen–Harrington under the direction of Van Dusen's son Frederick in partnership with Rochester native and Minneapolis businessman Charles. M. Harrington. By the turn of the century, it was

RESIDENCE OF GEO. W. VAN DUSEN, ROCHESTER, MINN

Above: Van Dusen House. *From* Andreas's Historical Atlas of the State of Minnesota, *1874.*

Left: Van Dusen mausoleum. *Photo by Paul David Scanlon.*

one of the world's largest grain dealers. The company became part of the Peavey Company, which was acquired by ConAgra (the nation's second-largest food company) in 1982. Also, in 1889, Van Dusen's other son Frank moved back to Rochester to farm on the south side of town and manage some of the family's financial interests.

In 1891 (when he was sixty-five), George had a twelve-thousand-square-foot residence and carriage house built in Minneapolis. The Van Dusen Mansion is a Richardsonian Romanesque design by Orff and Joralemon at 1900 LaSalle Avenue South in the Steven's Square neighborhood just southwest of the core of downtown Minneapolis. Nicknamed "The Castle" by locals, it has had a checkered history and was nearly demolished in 1994. It was restored in 1995–97 at a cost of over $1 million, and in 1995 it was added to the National Register of Historic Places. It was featured in the 2009 Coen brothers' film *A Serious Man*. In 2007, thirty-seven-year-old businessman Trevor Cook bought it for $2.6 million in cash to use as his office. In 2010, he pleaded guilty to swindling over nine hundred investors out of $158 to $194 million in a Ponzi scheme. He was sentenced to twenty-five years in prison. St. Paul attorney Jeff Anderson bought the mansion for $1.55 million in 2010, converted it to an events center and sold it to Tim George for $3 million in 2016. It now functions as a popular downtown venue for weddings and civic events.

Van Dusen died in Minneapolis on February 24, 1915. His body was interred in the mausoleum in Oakwood Cemetery.[30]

HORACE HORTON, 1867

Horace Ebenezer Horton was born in Western New York in 1843 and came to Rochester as a thirteen-year-old boy in 1856. After he finished the schooling available here in Rochester, he was sent back to New York for two more years of schooling. He was an excellent math student and studied engineering. Horton returned to Rochester and served as Rochester city engineer and Olmsted County surveyor. He started a successful construction business, building both commercial and residential buildings. When the courthouse was severely damaged by the 1883 tornado, Horton designed and built the renovation, including a new tower. Beginning in 1867, at the age of twenty-three, he showed a talent for bridge design and construction. His first bridge was a 186-foot timber span, 60 feet above the water, at

Frank's Ford Bridge at 90th Street NW. *Photo by Paul David Scanlon.*

Oronoco (background of image on page 27). By 1898, his firm had built seven bridges in Olmsted County and many more around Minnesota and surrounding states. The bridge at Frank's Ford (90th Street NW or County Road 121) is the sole remaining local Horton bridge. No longer used for automotive traffic, it is listed on the National Register of Historic Places.

In 1889, Horton moved to Chicago and founded the Chicago Bridge & Iron Co. (CB&I). It became nationally recognized for bridge and water tower design and construction. He managed it until his death in 1912. His grave in Oakwood Cemetery is marked by the second-largest obelisk (after the Brackenridge family marker). Nineteen years after his death, in 1931, CB&I designed and built the iconic ear of corn water tower for the Reid-Murdoch (Monarch, and later Libby, McNeil & Libby, then Seneca Foods) canning plant. After Horton's time, the company evolved to building aboveground storage tanks for the petrochemical industry. During World War II, CB&I built service vessels for the navy, including landing ship tanks (LSTs, such as those used at Normandy). The company existed until 2018, when it was acquired by McDermott International. In 2017, it employed over thirty-two thousand workers worldwide with annual revenue of $6.7 billion.

Horace Horton Obelisk memorial. *Photo by Paul David Scanlon.*

Horton was one of the investors who bought the Heaney Block in 1876, after which it was called Horton's Block (see page 33). When he married his wife, Emma, in 1873, he bought the lot at 627 College Street (4th Street SW) and built a large house for his family. The house was sold in 1890 to C.F. Massey, owner of the eponymous department store. The Bamber family bought it in 1907, and it was eventually razed in 1942 to create a parking lot for the Foundation House.[31]

CRIME, 1867

Comprehensive histories of Olmsted County were published in 1866, 1883 and 1910. All three authors were judges, so it's not surprising that they include details of crime in the early years. Like most crime, it is often surprising what trivial events precipitate ghastly crimes. By comparison with our contemporary criminal justice system, prison terms in the past were surprisingly short. Eaton gives the best organized sequence of presentations.[32] The murder of Frederick Ableitner is an illustrative example. Ableitner and his wife, described as an old German couple, farmed two miles west of St. Charles. John Whitman, thirty-five years old, lived in St. Charles. He believed Ableitner had a stash of gold worth $2,000. He recruited two young transients, Charles Edwards and George Staley, to assist in a robbery. On October 29, 1867, the trio knocked at the farmhouse. When Ableitner came to the door, Whitman knocked him down with a club, and Staley shot him four times with a pistol. Ableitner died a painful death over several hours. There was just $15 in the house at the time of the attack. The next day, Staley was arrested, but initial evidence was not sufficient to charge him, so he was released. Ironically, he was held in custody by Whitman, who was not yet suspected of the crime. As the investigation proceeded, all three left town. Whitman was tracked down by a detective while working in the forests of Michigan in mid-December. Staley was apprehended at a lumber camp in central Wisconsin in late December. Whitman pleaded guilty to third-degree manslaughter and was sentenced to eight years in prison. He became ill while in prison and was pardoned after two and a half years. Staley was charged with and convicted of first-degree murder, for which he was sentenced to be hanged. The governor commuted his sentence to a prison term. He was considered an exemplary prisoner, and after six and a half years, he was pardoned and did not reoffend. Edwards escaped to Texas and was never brought to justice.

THE SISTERS OF ST. FRANCIS, LOURDES ACADEMY AND ASSISI HEIGHTS, 1877

Assisi Heights is the motherhouse, or congregational headquarters, and home to the Sisters of the Third Order Regular of St. Francis Congregation of Our Lady of Lourdes of Rochester, Minnesota, a Roman Catholic congregation for religious women. There are hundreds of congregations of Franciscan Sisters worldwide. The Rochester order was founded in 1877 by Mother Mary Alfred Moes. A native of Luxembourg, she came to New York in 1851 and made her way west to Joliet, Illinois, where in 1864 she founded the Sisters of Saint Francis of Mary Immaculate. In 1877, a request was received to establish an academy at Waseca, Minnesota. Along with her birth sister, Sister Mary Barbara Moes, and twenty-three other Franciscan sisters, she came first to Waseca, then Owatonna, before settling in Rochester to establish a new teaching community of Franciscan Sisters in the same year. They founded the girls' Academy of Our Lady of Lourdes on West 5th Street (West Center Street) between North Hunter Street (5th Avenue NW) and Clark Street (6th Avenue NW). In the early years, they also founded an academy in Owatonna and seven parochial schools in the region. In later years, they operated dozens of elementary and high schools, plus the College of St. Teresa in Winona and several hospitals in eight different states and two other countries.

The Academy of Our Lady of Lourdes evolved over many years before Assisi Heights was built in the 1950s. The original academy building was designed by Winona architect C.G. Maybury and built by Winona contractor C. Bohn in 1877. It was seventy-two feet by forty-eight feet with three floors

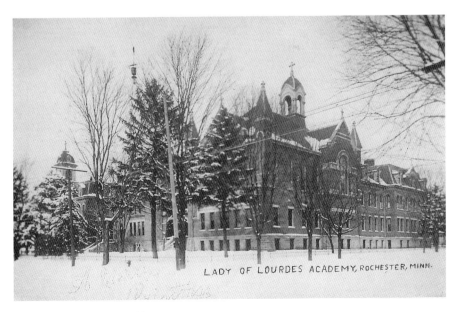

Lourdes Academy. *Postcard image.*

Assisi Heights. *Courtesy of Dean Riggott Photography.*

above a full basement. It housed an academy for high school–aged girls, Rochester's first parochial elementary school, a novitiate or training center for new sisters, living and dining quarters for the sisters, administrative space for the congregation of sisters and a chapel.

The congregation grew quickly and added to their motherhouse. The first addition was designed by C.G. Maybury & Son and constructed by (Martin) Heffron Construction Co. in 1888, the year before St. Mary's Hospital. It was 64 by 54 feet with floors and ceilings aligned, doubling the original space. The second addition, finished in 1908, was designed by E. Brielmaier & Sons of Milwaukee and built by Heffron Construction Co. It was *L* shaped in four segments totaling 86 feet by 178 feet, more than doubling space again. Over the years, the sisters acquired the entire block they occupied as well as the block to the west. There were a series of additional buildings that served various roles over the years, including St. Mary's Hall (1882) that was the girls' academy, an elementary school, a convalescent hospital, a music school, a convent, a rectory for the academy's chaplain and a heating plant and laundry building.

When Rochester was struck by a tornado on August 21, 1883, the sisters provided nursing care to many of the injured. Afterward, Mother Alfred was inspired to build a hospital for Rochester. She asked Dr. William Worrall

Mayo to be the medical director and staff it with his two sons. He reluctantly agreed, provided she raised the funds to build the hospital, which opened in 1889. I have never seen an account of the sources of funding she was able to tap. Mother Alfred died on December 18, 1899, in St. Paul at the age of seventy. Her obituary noted, "On the death of their parents they inherited a large fortune, which they devoted to that noble work they so generously undertook."[33] Mother Alfred and Dr. W.W. Mayo are considered the cofounders of Saint Mary's Hospital.

In 1894, the Sisters of St. Francis of Rochester founded a women's seminary in Winona, Minnesota. In 1907, under the leadership of Dr. Mary Molloy (1880–1954, Sister Mary Aloysius Molloy, OSF, after 1923), they founded the College of St. Teresa, a Catholic women's liberal arts college. It was operated successfully by the Sisters of St. Francis of Rochester, Minnesota, and was known particularly for its nursing program managed in cooperation with St. Mary's Hospital in Rochester. After its affiliated men's college, St. Mary's College of Winona, became coeducational in 1969, the College of Saint Teresa gradually lost enrollment and associated income. It modified its policies but never reversed its declining status. It closed in 1989, and the campus and buildings were sold to the Hiawatha Education Foundation (created by Robert Kierlin and cofounders of Fastenal Corporation to promote high-quality education in Winona). Portions of the former campus are now used by Cotter High School, Winona State University, St. Mary's University and several nonprofit arts organizations.

Rochester Catholic schools grew in the early twentieth century. Heffron High School, two blocks northwest of Central School next to St. John's Church, was built in 1913 but was gradually outgrown and became outdated. It was decided to build a central high school serving all parishes in the city, hence Lourdes Central Catholic High School was built and opened in 1942 on the block west of the academy. At the same time, the old motherhouse was badly overcrowded and in a poor state of repair. No adjacent land was available for expansion, so in 1949, the sisters purchased 138 acres (0.22 square miles) that consisted of a farm on the second-highest hill in town, plus the Walnut Hill estate of Dr. Louis Wilson with his house, 25-acre orchard, 7 acres of woods and extensive gardens. The site is one of at least three "Quarry Hills" in the city, with a panoramic view to the south centered on St. Mary's Hospital.

The sisters planned their "city seated on a hill." It was designed by Maguolo and Quick Architects and built by McCarthy Brothers Construction, both from St. Louis, Missouri. The cornerstone was laid on July 10, 1953. With an exterior clad in distinctive Mankato limestone with a red Spanish tile roof,

Assisi Heights is modeled after the Basilica of St. Francis in Assisi, Italy. It reflects the Italian Romanesque architecture of Umbria, the region where St. Francis of Assisi lived. It has a classical look, such that people often express surprise at the relatively recent dates of construction. The exterior is embellished with accents of granite from Norway, Sweden, Minnesota and Texas. The interior is Winona stone accented with marble from Spain, Italy, France, Morocco, Portugal, Yugoslavia, Belgium, Maryland and Tennessee. The floors are terrazzo. A decorative highlight is the entry lobby with twenty-four colored columns of five varieties of marble from Spain, France and Italy.

The sisters numbered nearly 800 in 1952 (and more than 1,000 in 1964), so Assisi Heights was designed as a 1,000-bed facility in six units, with living quarters for active sisters, a 50-room retirement facility for aging sisters, a 60-room hospital infirmary, a novitiate with housing and a college-level school with seven classrooms for 150 novices (those preparing to take the vows), an auditorium to seat 400, a retreat center with guest facilities for several hundred, a high-ceiling refectory (dining hall) to seat 500, kitchen and bakery, administrative offices for the religious order, common rooms, library, the main Chapel of Our Lady of Lourdes with stained glass by Emil Frei of St. Louis and seating for 500 and the smaller St. Clare Chapel, which seats 150. It contains 366 total bedrooms (95 for nursing and assisted living) and 288 other rooms (654 total rooms). It is configured in multiple wings in a boxed-eight shape with cloistered courtyards, up to five levels above ground and a basement. The front of the building is 450 feet long with total space of 385,342 square feet.

The laundry, garage and power plant were in a separate building on the north side, connected underground. (The laundry was since moved offsite.) Construction required two to three hundred workers (including thirty stonemasons) and took three years. The cost of construction was never publicized but reportedly was under budget. It was built to last at least one hundred years. It was dedicated on October 4, 1955. Since then, Assisi Heights has been the operational headquarters and living quarters, or "motherhouse," for the order.

As soon as Assisi Heights was finished, demolition of the old academy/motherhouse was begun. The site was cleared and regraded. In 1959, the site was sold to Mayo Clinic and has served for Mayo Clinic parking ever since. Two remaining outbuildings, St. Mary's Hall and St. Anthony Hall, were razed to make way for expansion of Lourdes High School in 1977 and 1983, respectively, the last remnants of the old building complex.

After the Second Vatican Council (1962–65), rules of the religious orders changed. Sisters were no longer required to wear habits, their traditional uniforms. Vocational options expanded. Some of the sisters continued their work in health care and education while some entered into areas of social service and advocacy for the poor. Sisters serve in eight states: Minnesota, California, Colorado, Illinois, Missouri, New Mexico, South Dakota and Texas. Mission work is being done in Colombia, where the Sisters have two schools and a clinic, and in Cambodia, where the Sisters founded a school to prepare men and women for careers in education. Currently, the order includes 145 professed Sisters of Saint Francis and 127 Cojourners (lay women and men in the broader community). A majority of the congregation is located in Rochester and a few other communities in Minnesota.

In addition to its role as the motherhouse of the Sisters of St. Francis and the retirement home for aging sisters, Assisi Heights is now a spiritual center for retreats and classes and provides space for a variety of religious organizations. Event spaces, such as the chapel, are available for public use. Public tours are available as allowed by infection control standards. After 2000, the sisters were faced with the possible loss of their motherhouse because of the declining numbers in their order, loss of income from St. Marys and the costs of operation and maintenance for the giant facility. They considered selling it. In 2009, Mayo Clinic signed an agreement with the Sisters to lease space in Assisi Heights for meetings, seminars and other functions. They initially leased 21,000 square feet with options to lease up to 100,000 square feet. Since then, Mayo Clinic has provided funding for needed capital improvements such as improved heating and air-conditioning. In some ways, this is a welcome renewal of the partnership between the Sisters of St. Francis and Mayo Clinic that was embodied in St. Marys Hospital for nearly one hundred years.[34]

Richard Sears from Stewartville and Spring Valley, 1886

Richard Warren Sears founded Sears, Roebuck & Company with his partner Alvah Curtis Roebuck. He was born on December 7, 1863, in Stewartville, Minnesota. In 1869, his family moved to Spring Valley, where he was friends with Almanzo Wilder, future husband of Laura Ingalls Wilder, as well as Fred and Kerry Conley (see Conley-Maass, pages 60–64). Sears's father died when he was seventeen, leaving him to provide for his mother and two sisters. He worked as a telegraph operator, then as a railroad station agent in

Redwood Falls, Minnesota. When a local jeweler refused a watch shipment, Sears accepted the shipment and sold the watches for a large profit. In 1886, with the proceeds, he started a mail-order business in Minneapolis called R.W. Sears Watch Company.

Sears hired Alvah C. Roebuck as a watch repairman and moved the business to Chicago. They joined as partners and expanded their business to other jewelry, then other dry goods, advertising by catalogue under the name Sears, Roebuck & Co. For a long time, Sears wrote the text for the catalogues himself. The mail order business grew steadily, then even more so with the advent of rural free delivery (1896) and parcel post (1913). The catalogue grew to over five hundred pages, shipped by the hundreds of thousands (later tens of millions), and became an icon of rural consumerism.

The company was plagued by poor shipping processes, slowing deliveries of orders. In 1895, Roebuck sold out to a brilliant businessman, Julius Rosenwald, who reorganized the company to improve its orders fulfillment processes. They built a three-million-square-foot distribution complex in Chicago in 1906 with vastly improved processes. Customer satisfaction and sales improved dramatically.

Sears House in Stewartville. *Courtesy of the History Center of Olmsted County.*

As Rosenwald gained increasing control of the company, Sears remained employed as the creative marketing force, but in 1909 his health was declining from chronic kidney disease. When Sears and Rosenwald had a disagreement over the advertising budget, Sears resigned as president and retired (at the age of forty-five) to a farm in Lake Bluff, Illinois, north of Chicago. He died on September 28, 1914, in Waukesha, Wisconsin, at the age of fifty-one. Sears's childhood home in Stewartville is listed on the National Register of Historic Places and is open to the public.

Sears opened its first retail store in Chicago in 1925, and six years later retail surpassed mail order sales. In the era of the Great Depression in the 1930s, Sears catered brilliantly to the thrift-minded consumer and nearly doubled its retail outlets in that decade. Sears was America's largest retailer and the standard for modest prices with good quality until the 1980s, when competition from Kmart, then Walmart and others, took away retail market share. Mail-order competitors also proliferated. A series of mergers, acquisitions and spinoffs muddied Sears' brand identity and aggravated its finances. Craftsman Tools, one of Sears's flagship brand names, was sold. They are now distributed by Lowe's. Retail and mail-order sales declined. In 2018, Sears Holdings filed for Chapter 11 bankruptcy protection. In February 2019, ESL Investments purchased Sears Holdings for $5.2 billion. At that time, 223 Sears stores remained open, but there are only 23 now, with dismal expectations for the future.

Sears opened its first retail store in downtown Rochester in 1936 at the southeast corner of Broadway and Center Street. In addition to a major downtown retail outlet, it had strong support for catalogue sales with a "Catalog Telethrift" support center. Sears was the first department store to vacate downtown Rochester and move to the outskirts when it opened its store at Crossroads Center south of "The Beltline" (U.S. Highway 14 or 12th Street S.) in 1963. It was a 55,000-square-foot retail facility with an auto service center and catalogue support center. In 1991, Sears moved to an even larger 113,000-square-foot facility at Apache Mall. It suffered the same influences locally as nationally and gradually declined in popularity. It closed in 2014.[35]

EYOTA LAMPLIGHTERS, 1893

In the 1893 election, licensing for saloons in Eyota was not approved as a "temperance" measure, making Eyota a "dry" town. Until then, revenue

Main Street, Eyota, Minnesota. *Postcard image.*

from saloon licenses provided the funds to maintain fuel for streetlights, and no provision had yet been made for alternate funds to maintain streetlights. When the lack of money for streetlights was pointed out, a temperance organization of young women raised funds by subscription and bought lamps and oil and with consent of the town council assigned each lamp to one of the women. They kept them lit regularly until the next regular election, at which time alternate funds were approved. The initiative of the women of Eyota was noted favorably by national publications, including the *Kansas City Star* and the *New York World*.[36]

CONLEY-MAASS BUILDING: CONLEY CAMERAS, MAASS PLUMBING AND WATERS CORPORATION, 1900

The history of the Conley-Maass/Downs/Bleu Duck Building is a complex slice of Rochester history. Antique collectors may be aware that the Conley Kewpie was a popular early consumer-friendly camera that competed with the Eastman (Kodak) Brownie and later the Polaroid Insta-Matic. Brothers Fred and Kerry Conley founded the Conley Camera Co. in 1899 in the back of their jewelry shop in Spring Valley. In 1903, Sears, Roebuck & Co. lost control of its camera supplier to Kodak. Richard Sears, who was born in Stewartville and moved to Spring Valley at the age of six, was a childhood friend of the Conley brothers. Sears contracted with the Conleys to manufacture its cameras. The following year, they moved their operations to a larger facility in Rochester at 14 West College Street (4th Street SW). Business grew rapidly, necessitating a move in 1909 to a much larger building at 501 North Main Street (1st Avenue NW). They produced up to twenty-eight thousand cameras per year and a variety of camera accessories. Between 1906 and 1910, Sears bought nearly half, then eventually all the stock in the company.[37] The Conley brothers moved on to other businesses. Kerry continued in business in Rochester, and his brother Frederick moved to Portland, Oregon, to start a cash register company.

The Conley Co. continued production of cameras, initially with dry plates and in 1913 the Conley Junior, their first camera using film supplied in rolls. In 1915, they introduced the Conley Kewpie, a simple camera to compete with the Kodak Brownie. Around that time, they began production of phonographic equipment. By 1927, they had stopped production of cameras, dropped the word *Camera* from the company name and expanded production of phonographs. Production grew rapidly with the Phonola, of which it produced seventy-five thousand in 1929.

In 1940, Sears, Roebuck & Co. sold the Conley Co. to Glen M. Waters, and the name was changed to the Waters Conley Co. It continued production of phonographs and also home milk pasteurizers. During World War II, the company produced electronic equipment for military applications in aviation and tanks, and in 1949, it diversified with a medical instruments division

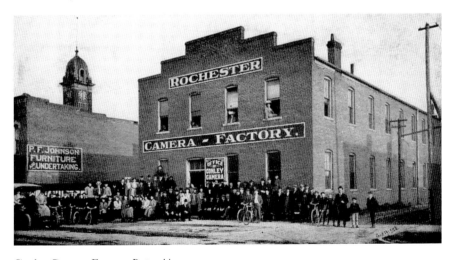

Conley Camera Factory. *Postcard image.*

focused on noninvasive measurement of cardiac and respiratory function.[38] In 1954, the company sold off the pasteurizer and phonograph production and became Telex Communications Inc. In 1957, Waters Corp. contracted with IBM for manufacture of cable assemblies and other electronics. Between 1961 and 1969, the company was a division of Flo-Tronics Inc. of Minneapolis. It acquired a manufacturer of electric fence chargers that accounted for 50 percent of sales versus 30 percent in electronic cable assemblies and the remainder in medical products. In 1971, Waters Instruments consolidated all operations in a new headquarters in Rochester. In 1974, Tom Burton took over as CEO from George Waters. Waters stepped down as chair of the board in 1990.[39] In 2005, the company was renamed Zareba Systems (an Arabic term for "cattle pen") to support the cattle fence business that accounted for 93 percent of sales in that year. Headquarters for that division are in Lancaster, Pennsylvania.[40] The smaller medical equipment and supply business is operated separately as Waters Medical Systems LLC in Rochester, Minnesota. It now produces systems and supplies for organ preservation for transplantation.[41] The 1909 Conley camera factory still exists at 501 1st Avenue NW, where it functions as a Mayo Clinic warehouse.[42]

The brick structure at 14 West College Street is 44 by 132 feet with two stories. It was originally built in 1900 to manufacture pants out of wool fabric produced by the Rochester Woolen Mills (see page 26). Construction was coordinated by a Connecticut entrepreneur named Henry K. Terry and funded by local investors in the mill. It was constructed by Martin Heffron (see the Heffron Brothers, pages 44–46). The mill and factory failed and declared bankruptcy in 1903, allowing the Conley purchase in 1904. Conley moved to the new factory in 1909. Maass and McAndrew Plumbing and Heating occupied the building from 1910 to 1955. It was subsequently home to Bob's Liquor, the Eagles, VFW, Waters Conley, City Loan & Finance, Salvation Army, Moose Lodge, Reichert's Appliance, Troy's Billiard Supply, Rochester Ballet School and Masque Theatre, Word Players Theater and Just for Kix.[43]

Ernest H. Maass Sr. (1865–1948) was born in Germany, immigrated to the United States at the age of eight and grew up in Winona. He was educated through sixth grade, then started to work, first as a tailor, then at a lumber mill. He came to Rochester in 1884 and worked for Clausen & Adler, then Parmele Hardware. Trained on the job, he mainly worked in sheet metal fabrication. He first met Dr. Will for treatment of "rheumatism" and later did some duct work for Dr. Will at the old Mayo house on Franklin Street (on the site of the Siebens Building), where the Mayo brothers lived in their early childhood. When St. Mary's Hospital was built, Parmele had the contract for plumbing and "tin work." In addition to the sheet metal work, Maass distinguished himself for fabricating foot-operated OR sinks for Dr. Will, a safety door for the elevator shaft and observation stands for visiting physicians in the ORs. In 1900, Maass joined in partnership with steamfitter Richard McAndrew. Maass must have been an extraordinary worker. He received spontaneous offers of financial backing from both of his former employers and from Dr. Will Mayo. Their business grew rapidly, doubling in volume almost annually. By 1911, the business employed thirty plumbers with projects throughout the region.

Maass and McAndrew performed most of the plumbing and heating work for the Mayo offices in the Massey building followed by the move to the Masonic Temple in 1901. Maass was tapped to fabricate most of the equipment for the pathology lab when Dr. Louis Wilson joined the staff in 1905. And when Dr. Henry Plummer began his work with X-rays, Maass fabricated both equipment and safety shields. In 1910, Maass and McAndrew incorporated and bought the building at 14 College Street. At a time when indoor plumbing was rare, Maass and McAndrew were the only plumbing business in town. A 75 percent increase in Rochester's population between 1910 and 1920 resulted in numerous large commercial contracts for new construction by the city, county, state hospital, schools, hotels, churches and so on, in addition to the growing Mayo practice and St. Mary's Hospital.

The aseptic surgical techniques that were key to the successful Mayo practice were heavily dependent on equipment and methods developed in conjunction with Maass and McAndrew. The ubiquitous "Mayo" instrument stands were designed and fabricated by Maass and McAndrew. They even produced spirometers for making respiratory measurements in Dr. Walter Boothby's lab.

St. Mary's was unable to keep up with demand for hospital facilities, so at the request of the Mayos, John Kahler built a series of downtown hospital/hotel hybrids to meet the demand, including the original Kahler (later renamed Damon Hotel), the Zumbro, the Colonial, the Stanley, the Worrall, the Curie and the new Kahler, all between 1907 and 1921. Maass and McAndrew managed the design and installation of plumbing, heating and ventilation and many of the mechanical systems.

Based on earlier work, Dr. Plummer had selected Ernest's son Fred Maass (1891–1955) as a young man to manage the design and installation of plumbing, heating and ventilation for the 1914 building. As Fred took over more of the management of the firm, Ernest Sr. began to step down toward retirement. Fred's role grew in relationship with the clinic leaders, particularly Dr. Plummer. In his role in the design of mechanical systems for the 1914 building, he produced a sophisticated central ventilation system, a central vacuum system, a gas incinerator, a pressure regulator for the water supply and an internal records delivery system (the "tube system"). Fred Maass continued to play a key role, along with Dr. Plummer and Ellerbe Architects, in the design of mechanical systems for the Franklin utilities plant and for the 1928 new clinic building (subsequently named the Plummer Building) and the system of dual tunnels that connected all the buildings belowground. The pneumatic tube system was designed in collaboration with the Lamson Corporation. It revolutionized the expeditious handling of medical records and specimens. In the current age of electronic medical records, the tube system is still in use for transporting physical records and specimens around the clinic campus. Fred Maass designed many custom features and devices for medical equipment as well.

In 1929, Fred Maass was offered and accepted a position as chief engineer for Mayo Clinic, a position he held for twenty-six years until he died at the age of sixty-four in 1955. He was responsible for all electrical and mechanical systems for the clinic, including planning for new facilities and design and fabrication support for the aeromedical research unit during World War II. His role was the start of the Division of Engineering at Mayo Clinic. Meanwhile, Maass and McAndrew continued to provide plumbing, heating, ventilation, air conditioning and mechanical systems to the growing clinic and city into the 1950s.[44]

In 2015, Traci and Hunter Downs purchased the Conley-Maass Building, and the city council established an economic development district and tax-increment financing with $400,000 toward funding for a $2.2 million historic restoration with a restaurant on the lower level and a series of small commercial incubators or office condominiums on the upper level.[45] The building was added to the National Register of Historic Places in 2016.[46] Bleu Duck was opened in August 2016 by owners Erik Kleven and Jennifer Lester. They have won numerous local awards for fine dining, including Best New Restaurant in 2017 and overall Best Restaurant in 2019 through 2023. They have adapted through the COVID pandemic with take-out and dine-in service and were awarded Best Dealing with a Pandemic Restaurant as well as Best Food Truck in 2021.[47] The upper-level office space is managed as coworking space by the Collider Foundation to foster innovation. In February 2021, they announced a tenant agreement with Google to house a new collaboration between Google and Mayo Clinic.[48]

Bank Robberies, 1900

In late May 1900, the safe of the Dover Bank was blown open at night and $4,500 was taken. One of the perpetrators was a notorious safe breaker, Thomas O'Neil, known as Omaha Kid. He was arrested in June in Chicago and was indicted in Olmsted County court on two counts of burglary. Tried in two separate trials, he was acquitted of the first but convicted of the second count and sentenced to four and a half years in prison. One of his associates in the robbery, James Johnson, aka Toronto Jimmy, was arrested in Juno, Wisconsin, in January 1901 and eventually extradited from Illinois in January 1903. While awaiting trial, he escaped from the local jail by cutting through steel bars over an outside window. He remained at large for over five years until October 1908, when he was arrested in Kentucky and charged with two bank robberies there. Two other associates, known as Lefty Fitzgerald and Daddy Flynn, were never charged.[49]

On December 4, 1926, a Saturday morning, a dramatic bank robbery occurred at the Olmsted County Bank and Trust Co. at 109 South Broadway. Shortly after the bank opened at 9:00 a.m., four to six armed men rushed into the bank and ordered the employees to lie down in the back of the building. The bank president, Charles Dabelstein, was knocked down and ordered to join the rest. The robbers were well organized and efficient. They quickly collected $70,000 in cash and bonds but left $5,000 in gold. An alarm was triggered but misinterpreted as a false alarm, delaying arrival of the police. Responding police exchanged gunfire with the robbers. Two officers were shot, but no one was killed. The robbers escaped in two waiting automobiles, which sped out of town without a trace. One of the robbers, Tony Serpa, was later identified from photographs of known suspects. The governor of Illinois refused extradition from Chicago, citing lack of evidence. Serpa was eventually extradited from St. Louis, Missouri, and tried in Olmsted County District Court on a charge of entering a bank with the intent to commit a felony. He was found guilty on May 16, 1929, and sentenced to life in prison. He entered prison on July 31, 1929, but was paroled eleven years later and released from prison on August 7, 1940. The other robbers were never identified or apprehended.[50]

In 1933, the State Bank of Byron was robbed twice. On March 17, 1933, a lone gunman, Frank Carpenter, took $3,400. He was not apprehended. On September 6, 1933, the bank was robbed by a lone gunman for the second time in six months. The thirty-year-old robber, Silva Speckeen, had been recently discharged from the army. He had previously served time in the state penitentiary for auto theft. He entered the bank in the afternoon when there were no other customers and only two employees. He herded the employees into a vault room. Two other women customers entered, both of whom he courteously escorted into the vault. Then, a sixty-eight-year-old farmer from Rock Dell named Charles Gronvold entered and spoke with the robber. Out of sight of the four women, a scuffle was heard, interrupted by a gunshot. Gronvold was shot through the heart and died immediately. The robber fled and drove away in a stolen car. A neighbor got the license number and a good description of the car. The robber was sighted south of St. Paul. While being pursued, he shot himself in the head. He died at a nearby St. Paul hospital after efforts to save him were unsuccessful.[51]

Rochester State Bank, near Miracle Mile, was robbed on March 15, 1971, by Robert John "Red" Ryan, a forty-one-year-old lone gunman. He entered the bank and told two assistant vice presidents to "fill up" two cloth bags. He took $30,965. As he left, he fired at one of the bank personnel who followed him. No one was injured. He fled in a car with police in pursuit. He was apprehended less than an hour later near Wasioja, twenty-two miles northwest of Rochester in Dodge County, after becoming stuck in deep snow in a farm field. $12,000 was recovered from a nearby stream, and a search was made for the remainder of the stolen money and the gun. On March 27, a federal grand jury indicted him for armed robbery.[52] He was tried in United States District Court for the District of Minnesota in 1971, found guilty and sentenced to fifteen years in federal prison, which he served in the United States Penitentiary at Leavenworth, Kansas. He was eligible for parole in 1976 after five years, but it was denied because of the severity of his offense (due to discharge of a firearm in the process).[53]

On the morning of August 30, 1978, Marquette Bank president John Chisholm received a call from an anonymous caller who instructed him to deliver $500,000 (in unmarked bills) in a briefcase to a Kahler elevator sent to the sixth floor. Failure to do so in thirty minutes would result in detonation of a bomb in the Marquette Bank lobby. Chisholm agreed, then notified the FBI, who instructed him to fill a briefcase with newspaper and make the delivery, which he did. He called the extortionist back to receive instructions for deactivating the bomb, but the caller said he didn't receive the briefcase and hung up on Chisholm. The bank building was evacuated and searched, but no explosives were found. The extortionist, Harry A. Skeen of Percy, Mississippi, was arrested by the FBI five days later. He was convicted and sentenced to six years in prison.[54]

On May 4, 1992, Scott Lee Weiss, twenty-three, of Rochester robbed Eastwood State Bank of $4,010 in cash. He fled the scene on a blue bicycle with the cash stuffed in plastic bags, after which he was known as the "Bicycling Bandit." He became a suspect when he quit his job and paid his overdue rent and bought new clothing using a thick wad of $10 bills. He was sentenced to eight years in federal prison.[55]

Bank robberies are rarely the source of comedy; however, a man, later identified as thirty-six-year-old Ryan Liskow, was caught after he robbed Sterling State Bank on Bandel Road NW twice on consecutive days. KIMT reporter Adam Sallet was broadcasting live from the scene on the day of the second robbery, December 15, 2015. As he was speaking, an employee of the bank ran out and told him that the same robber had just robbed the bank again and was immediately nearby. The robber was apprehended later the same day for driving a stolen vehicle. He was sentenced to nine and a half years in federal prison. Sallet became a YouTube celebrity with over four million views of the broadcast.[56]

BURT EATON, 1900

Burt Winslow Eaton was born in Jamestown, New York, on September 29, 1854; was moved as an infant to a farm in Cascade Township in 1855; and grew up in Rochester. He studied law under C.C. Willson and was admitted to the bar in 1879. In 1880, he opened a law office in partnership with Frank B. Kellogg on the second floor of the Horton (Heaney) Block (at the NW corner of Zumbro/2nd Street and Broadway). They both practiced successfully. Kellogg moved to St. Paul in 1887. Eaton served as city recorder from 1881 to 1887, Olmsted County attorney from 1887 to 1889 and mayor in 1898–99.

Eaton was a friend to Drs. Will and Charlie Mayo and, beginning around 1900, their legal counsel and financial manager. He managed all financial assets for them personally as well as for the Mayo practice. Eaton initiated Mayo Clinic's Legal Department, serving as the primary legal counsel to the organization for most of twenty years.

In 1917, the Mayos persuaded Judge George Granger to join Burton as legal counsel for the Mayo group. Together with Harry Harwick, they formed a committee charged by Dr. Will to create a legal entity that would ensure that the assets of the clinic "would be dedicated in perpetuity to

Burt Eaton. *Used with permission of Mayo Foundation for Medical Education and Research.*

the advancement of medical education and research." They recruited other legal minds to consult with them, including Pierce Butler, later a justice of the U.S. Supreme Court, and Fred B. Snyder, chair of the Board of Regents of the University of Minnesota. In Harwick's opinion, the greatest contribution came from Winona attorney Leslie L. Brown, whom Harwick called the "legal father of Mayo Properties Association." Brown's partner, Stephen H. Somsen, contributed substantially with the actual writing of the legal document. It was signed on October 8, 1919, creating the Mayo Properties Association (renamed Mayo Foundation in 1964).[57] Of the original Board of Trustees, Harwick, Eaton, Granger and Brown were the four non-physicians (along with Drs. Will and Charlie plus Drs. Plummer, Judd and Balfour).[58]

Eaton was the butt of a humorous story about W.W. Mayo. The "Old Doctor" was notoriously fast and impatient when driving his carriage on house calls. One snowy day, Burt Eaton hired a cutter with driver to take him to a neighboring town for a business call. They were passed by a faster carriage that drove them into the snowbank. Dr. Mayo waved as he passed. Eaton was indignant, but his driver assured him that all the local drivers yielded to the "Old Doctor." Nevertheless, he held the senior Mayo in the highest regard as a physician.

Among his many civic contributions, Eaton was the founding president of the Olmsted County Bar Association from 1894 until 1932, president of the Rochester Public Library board from 1895 to 1898, treasurer of the Rochester Cemetery Association from 1896 to 1941 and president of the Olmsted County Historical Society from 1926 until his death in 1941. He was president of the group that raised funds in 1911 to commission the memorial statue of W.W. Mayo, president of the Rochester Water Company, vice president of First National Bank for many years and also president of the Minnesota Bar Association in 1925. In 1926 (at age seventy-two!), he was appointed judge of municipal court and never retired. He served fifteen years until December 16, 1941, when he died following a brief illness at the age of eighty-six.[59]

DR. LOUIS WILSON, 1905

Louis B. Wilson was the founding head of the Section of Pathology of Mayo Clinic and is best remembered for developing the "frozen section procedure," a rapid method to prepare samples of surgical biopsies for immediate diagnosis during surgical procedures. This allowed surgeons to make operative decisions while their patients were in the operating room, such as wide excisions or lymph node dissections for malignancies versus limited procedures for benign conditions. Without such intraoperative feedback, earlier surgeons had performed operations for malignancy in multiple stages to allow the time needed for pathological review. Wilson developed and published his method in his first year at Mayo Clinic, 1905. It quickly became, and remains, the standard for intraoperative management and contributed to the operative successes of the Mayo brothers and their colleagues.[60]

Wilson was born in Pittsburgh in 1866. He graduated from a Pennsylvania teacher's college in 1886 and taught high school biology in St. Paul for eight years before receiving his medical degree from the University of Minnesota in 1896. He worked for nine years for the Minnesota State Board of Health in its bacteriology laboratory while teaching bacteriology at the University of Minnesota.

He was recruited to the Mayo group in 1905 to organize and expand its laboratories. The next twenty years were a time of significant growth for Mayo Clinic and major expansion in the number and complexity of medical

Right: Dr. Louis Wilson.
*Used with permission of
Mayo Foundation for Medical
Education and Research*.

Below: Wilson House.
*Courtesy of Dean Riggott
Photography*.

laboratory methods. From 1905 to 1924, surgical procedures increased by more than sixfold, meanwhile laboratory space increased from 3 rooms to 135 rooms plus an animal hospital and a 360-acre farm. Laboratory staff increased from 2 to 263, including 66 physicians and scientists engaged in general pathology, clinical pathology, surgical pathology, bacteriology, biochemistry, hematology, serology, metabolism, experimental surgery, biophysics, necropsy service, gastric analysis, urinalysis, electrocardiography, photography, medical illustration, roentgenography, radiation physics and a research museum.

Wilson became an expert in the pathology of thyroid diseases and in the use of medical photography. He developed other areas of expertise, including the effects of bullet wounds on tissues, a timely topic during World War I. He was an expert marksman and used a private firing range on his property on Walnut Hill (now known as Assisi Heights) to study ballistics. In 1918–19, he served as assistant director of the Laboratory Division of the American Expeditionary Forces in Europe. He was promoted to colonel and received the Distinguished Service Medal.

In addition to his leadership in laboratory medicine and pathology, Wilson was an educational leader. He was director of Mayo Foundation for Medical Education and Research (effectively Mayo Clinic's first dean for education) from 1915 until his retirement in 1937. During his tenure, Mayo Graduate School of Medicine was created and quickly became the largest postgraduate medical education program in the world. He served as president of the American Association of Medical Colleges (1931–32) and president of the American Board of Medical Specialties (1935–37).

Wilson was married three times. He married Mary Stapleton in 1891. She died in 1919 after a prolonged illness. He married Maud Headline Mellish in 1924. She died in 1933. He then married Maud's close friend Grace McCormick in 1935. They lived in three historic houses in Rochester. Louis lived in an Ellerbe-designed house at 830 4th Street SW from 1909 until 1925. Maud lived briefly in an Ellerbe-designed house at 799 3rd Street SW from 1923 until 1924 or 1925. She married Louis in 1924, and together they moved to their new Harold Crawford–designed house at 1001 14th Street NW on top of Walnut Hill in 1925. Its extensive grounds allowed Dr. Wilson to indulge his horticultural interests with extensive gardens and a twenty-five-acre orchard with 1,375 apple trees. Louis lived there with Grace after Maud's death in 1933. He died of amyotrophic lateral sclerosis in 1943 and is buried together with Maud and Grace in Oakwood Cemetery.[61]

MAUD MELLISH WILSON
(AND GRACE MCCORMICK WILSON), 1907

Annie Maud Headline was born on February 14, 1862, on a farm near Faribault, Minnesota, the daughter of Swedish immigrants. An exceptional student, she attended local country schools through age sixteen, then an academy in Medford, Minnesota, for one year. She considered a career in medicine but lacked the finances for medical school, so in 1885, at age twenty-three, she started nurse's training in Chicago at Presbyterian Hospital, where she had the opportunity to audit courses in Rush Medical School. She graduated in May 1887 and worked first as a private duty nurse, then became superintendent of Maurice Porter Memorial Hospital for Children. On September 28, 1889, she married a surgeon, Dr. Ernest J. Mellish. They moved to Ishpeming, Michigan, where he practiced until 1893, then returned to Chicago. They struggled financially during the recession that followed the Panic of 1893. She helped revise her husband's medical articles for publication and quickly established her considerable editing skills. At her husband's request, she dropped the name Annie and thereafter went by Maud Mellish. Ernest suffered from chronic tuberculosis but had a remission from 1897 to 1901, during which they relocated to El Paso, Texas. He died of tuberculosis in 1905, leaving Maud a widow after sixteen years of marriage. She moved back to Chicago and found employment as a librarian for Augustana Hospital and editor for Dr. Albert Ochsner, a close friend and correspondent of the Mayo brothers. In 1907, the Mayos recognized their need for a better organized library to support their burgeoning practice. Dr. Will inquired of Dr. Ochsner if he could recommend a librarian. Dr. Ochsner charitably recommended Mellish. Dr. Will implored her to consider their offer despite her hesitancy to return from Chicago to rural Minnesota.

On March 1, 1907, she began working for the Mayos organizing the library. She collected and organized the few books they had, sought advice and funds to purchase needed textbooks and set about retrieving and organizing medical papers already produced by the Mayo associates. They were in horrible disarray, necessitating her rescue of some reprints from storage in a coal bin.

It was readily apparent that the writing style and editorial quality of papers produced by Mayo-affiliated physicians, including the Mayos themselves, were variable at best and poor in most instances. Mellish gravitated to the role of editor and was given full control of editing for papers by Mayo

Maud Mellish Wilson.
Used with permission of
Mayo Foundation for Medical
Education and Research.

physicians. She was autocratic as an editor, described as a "tough critic." Many of the staff took umbrage at her mandated intrusion, but she had the full support of the Mayos. There was little dispute that the writing quality of papers from Mayo staff improved dramatically under her strict editorial watch. One apocryphal story claimed that Dr. Charlie submitted a paper to Mellish for editing. When he read the revision, he did not recognize the paper as his own.

By 1909, the practice had outgrown the small office library in the Masonic Temple. A separate two-story structure was built to the west of the Masonic Temple to house the library and the beginnings of the Section of Medical Illustrations, which also fell under Mellish's control.

In 1914, the Section of Publications was established under her leadership on the third floor of the new red brick building. It included an editorial section, the library and an art studio. A full-time librarian allowed her to concentrate on editing. In 1922 she published a book, *The Writing of Medical Papers*, which went through three editions and was widely used. It included advice such as "When writing a medical paper, don't always go back to the Garden of Eden and review the literature to date." Also,

Grace McCormick Wilson. *Used with permission of Mayo Foundation for Medical Education and Research.*

"Don't forget that skipping about from tense to tense in one paragraph has not even a Bergsonian justification. It is blasphemous, ungrammatical, and annoying."

When the "New Clinic," subsequently called the Plummer Building, was finished in 1928, it housed the library, with twenty thousand volumes, plus a comprehensive journal collection, on the twelfth floor. Mellish continued as chief editor of the Section of Publications despite continuing controversy over her autocratic style. However, she had full support from "the chief" (Dr. Will) throughout her career at Mayo. She edited the "Collected Papers from the Mayo Clinic and the Mayo Foundation" from 1909 to 1933. She inaugurated the "Proceedings of the Staff Meetings of the Mayo Clinic" in 1926 (which became Mayo Clinic Proceedings). She organized eleven volumes of the *Surgical Clinics of North America* and twelve volumes of the *Medical Clinics of North America*. Over the course of her twenty-six years at Mayo, it is estimated that she edited six thousand papers for Mayo physicians and scientists. Dr. Will considered her the fourth-most influential person in the development of the clinic (after the Mayo brothers and Henry Plummer).[62]

She married Dr. Louis B. Wilson in 1924. He was director of the Division of Laboratories as well as Mayo Graduate School of Medicine. His first wife died in 1919 after a lengthy illness. In 1925, they built a new house designed by Harold Crawford on a fifty-acre plot on the top of what they referred to as Walnut Hill, between what are now Assisi Heights and Indian Heights Park. There he also developed extensive orchards, other resources for plant husbandry, a photography lab and facilities, including a gun range for his study of ballistics and war wounds of which he was an expert.

In October 1932, Mellish underwent an exploratory laparotomy revealing extensive abdominal carcinomatosis. She was treated with radiation but died on November 6, 1933. After Maud's death, Louis's third wife, Grace McCormick Wilson, established the Maud Mellish Wilson Memorial Playground on Walnut Hill as a half-day socializing activity for preschool children of Mayo employees. Grace was a child educator and a longstanding friend of Maud from Chicago.[63] Maud, Louis and Grace are buried together as a threesome in Oakwood Cemetery under a headstone that symbolically depicts their relationships with one another.

Wilson gravestone. *Photo by Paul David Scanlon.*

Mabel Root and Mayo Clinic Medical Records, 1907

The Mayo Clinic unified medical record system was inaugurated on July 19, 1907, with patient number A-1. New clinic numbers have been issued serially since then. Before this system, outpatient records were kept by individual physicians in large ledgers, and hospital and surgical records were kept at the hospitals in casebooks. Dr. Henry Plummer joined the Mayos in 1901. He sought a better system of recordkeeping. He studied other systems of medical records and other record models in business and industry. He proposed a dossier system based on a unique identifying number for each patient, issued serially. Each file would contain all inpatient and outpatient narrative and data and laboratory records for each individual patient, together in a single file, filed by patient number, in a central location from which it could be retrieved at any time by whoever needed it. He met some initial resistance, but soon all agreed the new system was an improvement on the old.

Mabel Root. *Used with permission of Mayo Foundation for Medical Education and Research.*

When the system was started, returning patients who had received care before the start of the new system were issued new numbers in sequence, and their previous records were collected from various sources and incorporated into the new file. The original plan was to batch the records in groups of 100,000, each beginning with a prefix letter, hence the *A*. That idea was abandoned in favor of serial numeration. The one millionth patient was registered in January 1938. Currently, new registration numbers are over 14-000-000.

Henry Plummer is given most of the credit for designing the system. It is often called the "Plummer system," but it was his assistant, Mabel Root, who worked out most of the details of the system and managed the system in its early days. Thus, it is more appropriately called the "Plummer-Root" system. In the earliest years, a great deal of searching was needed to find all the old data to incorporate into the new record system. When clinic records lacked previous surgical information, Root often traveled to St. Mary's to find the necessary information in surgical logs or in the billing office.

Beginning in 1908, Dr. Plummer and Root devised and implemented the indexing system for identifying the records by both major diagnoses as well as surgical procedures. Using five-by-eight-inch index cards, Root manually entered patient information, including patient number, date, age and sex on each card, for a given diagnosis or surgical procedure. Each five-by-eight card could identify hundreds of patients. This system allowed records to be searched for research purposes. This was a critical resource for developing innumerable clinical research studies for which Mayo Clinic became and remains famous.[64]

The system worked well from its beginnings and scaled well to much larger numbers of patients over the years. A commentary in 1926 noted that the system worked as well for 60,000 patients per year as it had for 5,000 per year in 1907.[65] That comment is still true nearly one hundred years later with over 14 million patients. Between 1907 and 1935, Root and her assistants manually indexed 880,000 patients with up to twenty diagnoses and procedures per patient. In 1935, the system was automated with a Hollerith punch card–based index designed by Dr. Joseph Berkson (see Rochester Epidemiology Project, pages 149–50). That system worked for forty more years until it was replaced by a computer database.

The use of a centralized unified medical record with organization of patients by serial number remains central to the current Mayo Clinic patient record system. In the days of the physical file, before conversion in the 1990s to an all-digital electronic medical record, the records used a unique paper size, commonly called "Plummer paper," that was slightly larger than legal size in both height and width. Only high-quality acid-free paper was used along with ink that would not fade over time. The old physical documents are still legible and retrievable, when needed, from warehouse storage.

Mabel C. Root (1878–1981) was born on January 5, 1878, near Rochester (in Marion), the daughter of a grocer who migrated to Rochester from central Minnesota during the Dakota War in 1862. Her mother died when she was sixteen, forcing her to quit high school and go to work. She was childhood best of friends with Daisy Berkman, the niece of Dr. Will and Dr. Charlie, who married Henry Plummer. Root met Henry before he and Berkman married. In 1907, when Henry needed an assistant for his medical records project, he hired Root. Her only prior work experience was as a clerk at E.A. Knowlton's dry goods store for thirteen years. She worked with him to devise the medical record system and managed it for many years as the supervisor of the Division of Records and Statistics, reporting to Maud Mellish Wilson and Dr. Plummer. As a close friend of both Daisy and Henry, she often worked at the Plummers' house in the evenings, particularly in the early days, working out the details of classification of diagnoses and surgical procedures for the indexing system. She remained a close friend of the Plummers.

Root retired in 1946 after a thirty-five-year career at Mayo Clinic, during which 1.2 million patients were registered and indexed. She lived in her house on W. Center Street until the age of 91. Then she moved nearer to her nieces and nephews in Minneapolis, still living independently past her 100th birthday. She died on August 1, 1981, at the age of 103. She never married or had children, but her grandnieces and nephews remain devoted to maintaining her legacy.[66]

HARRY HARWICK, 1908

Until 1901, Dr. Will Mayo managed the business aspects of the practice of the Mayo partnership with the assistance of caretaker Jay Neville. This included collections, bookkeeping, purchasing, banking and payroll. It was in disarray, particularly collections. In 1901, he asked for help from William Graham, a semiretired grocer and businessman in his late fifties. Graham was the elder brother of Dr. Christopher Graham and Edith Graham Mayo, Dr. Charlie's wife. Graham assisted without major reorganization, continuing the standard use of individual ledgers for accounting for each of the physicians in the practice and a haphazard method of individual collections by the physicians themselves.

Harry Harwick. *Used with permission of Mayo Foundation for Medical Education and Research.*

In 1908, Dr. Will decided the group needed someone to build a better accounting and business system for the practice, so he inquired of the president of the First National Bank, who recommended a promising twenty-one-year-old bank clerk. After a brief interview at the Mayo offices in the Masonic Temple, Dr. Mayo offered the job as Graham's assistant to Harry J. Harwick. Harwick began by upgrading the business ledgers to a loose-leaf ledger card system. Meeting with some resistance, he allied with Dr. Henry Plummer, who was attempting to introduce a unitary medical record system. Together they achieved the introduction of both. Harwick centralized purchasing, accounting and later collections. His tasks grew

Harwick family. *Used with permission of Mayo Foundation for Medical Education and Research.*

quickly with planning and construction of the 1914 red brick Mayo Clinic building, the establishment of Mayo Foundation for Medical Education and Research in 1915 and Mayo Properties Association in 1919. He became a trusted advisor to Dr. Will Mayo, "The Chief." In 1918, when Dr. Will developed hepatitis, his jaundice was initially assumed to be due to cancer. Dr. Will and Harwick spent the better part of the next two months conveying Dr. Will's long-term vision of how the organization should evolve. They took almost daily hours-long drives in the country in Dr. Will's car to discuss business management along with a broad range of other topics.

Harwick grew continually in his role as the first chief administrative officer of Mayo Clinic during his forty-four-year career, as detailed in his autobiography. He says that having organized Mayo Foundation for Medical Education and Research (Mayo Graduate School) and Mayo Properties Association, the next step was to arrange the internal management of the organization. That was done by the establishment of the Board of Governors and the committee organization.[67] Harwick was secretary and treasurer for Mayo Properties Association (later called Mayo Foundation) from 1919 to 1939. When Dr. Will died in 1939, Harwick was the only nonfamily member who attended him on his deathbed. At Dr. Will's insistence, Harwick succeeded Dr. Will as board chair and CEO until his retirement in 1953.[68] In 1960, Mayo Clinic named its new building for administration and records the Harwick Building.

Harwick was public minded as well. He was a principal proponent of the Rochester Foundation, the Kiwanis Club and the Rochester Rotary Club. He was instrumental in the creation of Kahler Corporation and numerous other local, state and national organizations.

Harry Harwick was born on a farm near Elk River, Minnesota, on September 2, 1887. He graduated from Winona High School in 1906. He married Margaret Graham, daughter of his boss William Graham, in 1910. After 1921, they lived at the apex of Pill Hill in a Georgian-style Ellerbe-designed house at 912 8th Street SW. They also had, after 1938, an Ellerbe-designed lake home on Lake Allis (Lake Shady) on the same property where the Mayo brothers once had their cottage. They had three children: J. William "Bill" Harwick, who became a Mayo Clinic administrator; Margaret Harwick Herrell; and Mary Anne Harwick Sundberg. They had twelve grandchildren. Harry Harwick died of a stroke on February 11, 1978, at the age of ninety. The massive ornate bronze doors of the Plummer Building were closed in his honor, the eighth person to be so honored.

The Harwicks' son, Bill, a 1935 graduate of Dartmouth, was hired by Dr. Will in 1937 to join the administration of Mayo Clinic. He served as secretary of Mayo Clinic Board of Governors from 1953, the year Harry Harwick retired, until his own retirement in 1976. He was chief administrative officer from 1970 to 1976 after Slade Schuster retired. The Harwicks' daughter Margaret married a Mayo Clinic–trained internist, Dr. Wallace E. Herrell. Their son, John Herrell, a Harvard Business School graduate, joined Mayo Clinic administration in 1968 and became chief administrative officer from 1993 to 2001, retiring one hundred years after Will Mayo hired his great-grandfather William Graham.[69]

Garfield Schwartz, 1909

Garfield Schwartz was the general contractor for Mayo Clinic in its early years. He was born in LaCrosse, Wisconsin, in 1880. He learned the construction trade while working for Noble Construction in Wisconsin. He came to Rochester in 1909 and established his own business, G. Schwartz

& Co., in partnership with his brother John. Their first contracts were the construction of a nursing facility at the Rochester State Hospital and the new Conley camera factory. His first work with the Mayos was as general contractor for Mayowood beginning in 1910. At Dr. Charlie's prompting, they used a poured reinforced concrete method for constructing the house. It was innovative and ultimately successful. Schwartz gained the trust of the Mayos and constructed every Mayo Clinic building from the 1914 building until he and John both retired in 1948. G. Schwartz & Co. was the main developer of College Hill after 1910 as it quickly became known as Pill Hill because of the predominance of Mayo Clinic physicians among the new homeowners.

Garfield Schwartz. *Used with permission of Mayo Foundation for Medical Education and Research.*

Schwartz recommended a professional architect for each project, most often Harold Crawford or the Ellerbe firm from Minneapolis. G. Schwartz & Co. built eleven houses on old College Street (4th Street SW) and many others in Pill Hill, including Garfield's own houses at 621 9th Avenue SW (1925) and 803 8th Street SW (1928) and John's houses at 828 8th Street SW (1922) and 503 6th Street SW (1927). G. Schwartz & Co. was the developer for Belmont Slope, a neighborhood built on a fifty-four-acre parcel from the Plummer estate sold by Daisy Plummer after Henry Plummer died in 1936. It includes Plummer Circle and Plummer Lane SW and 10th Street SW. It was also called Quarry Hill Neighborhood. During Garfield's thirty-eight-year career, he had contracts in the Dakotas, Iowa, Illinois, Michigan and Washington. In 1948, they sold the business to O.A. Stocke & Co. Schwartz's final home, designed by Crawford, is at 1127 7th Street SW (1954). He died in 1956. He and his wife, Selma (1888–1972), are buried in Oakwood Cemetery.[70]

ZOOS: MAYO PARK, BEFORT AND ZOLLMAN, 1907

Mayo Park began as a forty-acre parcel of land donated by the Mayo family to the city in 1907. It had a small zoo on the east side of the river

Reminders of Pioneer
Days, as preserved in
▆▆▆▆▆▆▆▆
Rochester, Minn

Copyright 1914 by C. A. Holland.

Mayo Park Zoo. *Postcard image.*

from 1911 until 1941. The zoo had a variety of animals, including bears, wolves, foxes, deer, elk and monkeys. Bison from Yellowstone Park were added in 1926. In 1937, late in the Depression, the bison were shot and sold for their meat. In 1941, as part of the war effort, the city attempted to give away the bears to another zoo, without success, so the bears were also shot and the zoo was closed. The Dee log cabin was kept on the site from 1911 until 1962, when it was moved to 3rd Avenue SW near the public library and the old History Center.[71]

The Befort Zoo was privately operated by Willard E. Befort from 1951 to 1954. It was on South Broadway/U.S. 63, three miles south of the edge of town, which was around 20th Street then. It included a lion, a tiger, a leopard, a cougar, a bobcat, monkeys, bears, deer, elk, bison, yaks, peccaries, eleven types of birds (including a bald eagle) and two snake species. Befort developed health problems in 1954. He sold out to a nonprofit group headed by William Van Hook (who was the city parks superintendent). The group hoped to form a Rochester Zoological Association and operate the zoo as an "educational as well as an amusement attraction," but it closed a year later. It is said that a zoo visitor had his hand mauled by the lion when he attempted to pet it. Concerns about liability may have contributed to the demise of the zoo. Befort retired to Dade City, Florida, where he died in September 1960.[72]

Zollman Zoo is in Oxbow Park, part of the Olmsted County Parks system. The park is 3 miles north of Byron on County Road 105. Oxbow Park is named for a bend in the South Branch of the Middle Fork of the Zumbro River. The park was started in 1967 with the purchase of 465 acres and expanded with the purchase of 107 additional acres in 1974 and the donation of 52 acres in 1998 (total 624 acres or 0.975 square miles). It has 8 miles of hiking trails, including hills of moderate difficulty, six picnic areas, four with shelters, twenty-nine camping sites, a historic farmhouse, a retreat facility and ski trails. The zoo was started in 1969 with donated native animals. It now exhibits over thirty species of Minnesota wildlife (mammals, large birds, snakes, eagles, owls, river otters, black bear, wolf, coyote, bison, elk, bobcat, cougar, lynx, badgers, prairie dogs) and a few domestic animals. It is named in honor of Dr. Paul E. Zollman, a Mayo Clinic veterinarian who provided his services to the zoo for many years. The nature center, adjacent to the zoo, was completed in December 1981. It offers educational programs throughout the year.

"MOONLIGHT" GRAHAM, 1909

Archibald Wright Graham was born on November 12, 1876, in Fayetteville, North Carolina. He played minor league baseball for seven seasons (1902–8) with teams from North Carolina, New England and New York. Known as "Moonlight" Graham, he was acquired in 1905 by the New York Giants, for whom he played in only one game on June 29. He played the ninth inning in right field but did not bat, and when he was fielding, no ball was hit to right field—thus, his recorded "stats" were all 0. It was his only major league appearance. His baseball career was fictionalized in the novel *Shoeless Joe* and in the movie *Field of Dreams*.

He received his medical degree from the University of Maryland in 1905 and continued with postgraduate training at Johns Hopkins. In 1909, he began his medical practice in Chisholm, Minnesota. He served on the staff of Rood Hospital in Chisholm until he was hired as Chisholm school physician in 1915, a position he kept for forty-four years. He maintained an interest in pediatric diseases, particularly eye diseases. He personally monitored blood pressures in over 100,000 schoolchildren and published observations from thirteen years of serial observations. He was a continual benefactor of poor children, providing medical care and glasses free

Gravestone of Dr. Archibald "Moonlight" Graham and Alecia Graham. *Photo by Paul David Scanlon.*

of charge to many schoolchildren. Townspeople described him as the personification of the beloved small-town doctor. He corresponded with the Mayo brothers and received continuing education through many trips as a visiting physician at Mayo Clinic.

He is not known to be related to the family of Dr. Christopher Graham. In 1915, he married Alicia Madden (1886–1981) of Viola Township. They had no children. He died on August 25, 1965 (aged eighty-eight), in Chisholm, Minnesota, and is buried in Calvary Cemetery (Section 9, Row 4)[73] in Rochester, Minnesota, alongside his wife.[74] Anonymous admirers leave baseballs and coins on his gravestone.

II

BETWEEN THE WARS (1914–1945)

Harold Crawford, 1916

For anyone with an interest in architecture in Rochester, the name Harold Crawford is preeminent, rivaled only by the Ellerbe firm in terms of both design aesthetic and number of buildings. Crawford had a long and distinguished career as a Harvard-trained and highly regarded architect. His style was diverse, and each building was unique. His buildings are among the most cherished and valued in Rochester.

"The man who wrote the book" on Crawford, Ken Allsen, actually wrote two books. The first, *Houses on the Hill: The Life and Architecture of Harold Crawford*, was published in 2003 by Noah Publishing of Kenyon, Minnesota. Allsen learned quite a bit more about Crawford afterward and identified a number of houses and other buildings designed by Crawford, an increase from 140 to 180 items. In addition, his first publisher went out of business. When time came to consider a reprint, Allsen decided on a different title and substantially upgraded content. The new book, titled *Master Architect: The Life and Works of Harold Crawford*, was published by the History Center of Olmsted County and printed by Davies Printing of Rochester, Minnesota, in 2014 with a grant from the Southeastern Minnesota Arts Council funded by the Clean Water Land & Legacy Amendment. I would advise anyone with more than a passing interest in local architecture to read Allsen's books.

Harold was born during a violent blizzard on April 6, 1888, in Beaver Creek, a rural frontier town in Southwest Minnesota. He was the younger of

Left: Harold Crawford.
Courtesy of the History Center of Olmsted County.

Opposite, top: Second Rochester Public Library, now Mayo Clinic Alix School of Medicine. *Postcard image*.

Opposite, bottom: U.S. Post Office (1934). First Street SW between 3rd and 4th Avenues (demolished 1978). *Postcard image*.

two sons of Frank Crawford, a local farmer, and his wife, Carrie Seymour, a native of Olmsted County who grew up in Orion Township near Eyota. Frank was a gambler who gave up on farming and moved the family to Seattle. In 1890, he abandoned his wife and family to go to Alaska. Lacking other options, Carrie moved back to her family farm and raised her sons there under impoverished conditions. Her aspirations for her sons were frustrated by poor-quality education in the rural school. Both boys failed to qualify by examination for transfer to Rochester schools, so Carrie arranged for Harold to live with her sister Lucy and her husband in South Dakota. For a year, he had much better educational opportunities and also worked at his uncle's newspaper. By the end of the year, his mother had moved to Rochester and purchased a rooming house. Harold moved back and enrolled in Rochester High School together in the same class with his older brother, Allen. Harold graduated as the top student in 1908.

That fall, he enrolled in the School of Architecture at the University of Illinois in Chicago, where his role models included Louis Sullivan and Frank Lloyd Wright. His advisor, who became a lifelong friend, was Frederick M. Mann. While in Chicago, he also gained practical experience working part

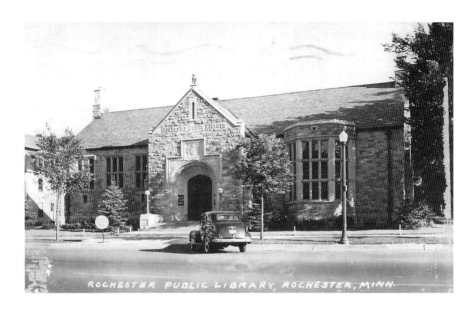

time as a draftsman for Chicago architectural firms and for a publisher of atlases. He graduated with a bachelor of art and architecture degree in 1913.

From there he went to Harvard to pursue a master's degree in architecture. With the support of Professor Mann, he received scholarship support at Harvard. While at Harvard, he also worked part time as a draftsman for two prominent architects from whom he learned a great deal. In the spring of 1916, Crawford received his Master of Art and Architecture degree from

Harvard and was advised by both his dean and his mentor to enter solo practice to develop his style independently. With opportunity to settle and prosper in virtually any city, he chose to return to Rochester to support his mother in her later years.

Harold's practice took off quickly, partly due to recommendations from his mentor, Frederick Mann. His first commission was an elegant horse barn for Dr. Christopher Graham, which still stands today off South Broadway, south of 9th Street SE. It is usually called the "chick hatchery." Graham immediately commissioned Crawford to design a major remodelling of the Lowry/Brackenridge/Graham house on Dubuque Street (813 3rd Avenue SE, see pages 29–31). In less than a year, he established a substantial local résumé.

During that same interval, Harold met his future wife at Calvary Episcopal Church. May Fisher was a native of Kentucky whose operatic voice took her all the way to the Berlin Opera, where she sang the lead role of Isolde in *Tristan und Isolde* in 1914. Sadly, the outbreak of World War I cut her career short, and she returned to the United States. On the returning steamship, she became quite ill but was cared for by Dr. Georgine Luden, a German pathologist who was traveling to join the staff of Mayo Clinic. Luden invited Fisher to join her entourage to Rochester, and she accepted rather than return to a teaching position in Cincinnati near her hometown. She joined the church choir and captured Crawford's notice with her soaring voice. Not long after that, he proposed marriage.

In the spring of 1917, Crawford joined the army as a second lieutenant. He hoped to travel overseas but was assigned to a base near Jacksonville, Florida, where he was responsible for developing plans for new army bases and instructing others to do likewise. His co-instructors were experienced construction professionals from whom he learned many practical aspects of the building trades.

In 1918, while Harold was in Florida, a woman named Rheta Lindow came to Rochester accompanied by her mother. She had terminal cancer and was pregnant. She was befriended and taken in by Dr. Luden, who proposed that May and Harold adopt the baby after Rheta's inevitable death. All parties agreed, including Rheta's estranged husband (the baby's biological father) and her mother. On June 29, Rheta delivered her baby at home assisted by Dr. Luden and May. When she was presented with the baby, she took her, named her Margaret Judd and passed her back to May, saying, "This is your baby now." Rheta died a short while later. Harold and May were married on September 10, 1919, after Harold's discharge from the army. Margaret Judd Crawford was adopted, effective November 1920. Though initially frail, she flourished under the Crawfords' care.

Harold's practice took off swiftly after the war. College Hill became known as Pill Hill and was developed over the years of his career. He was a preferred architect working with G. Schwartz & Co., the principal developer of Pill Hill (see pages 80–81). Crawford partnered with other architects on occasion but mostly worked alone and always did his own drafting. He had a close friendship with Edgar Buenger ("Bing" to friends), who was a principal associate of the Ellerbe firm as manager of its Rochester office. Buenger designed many of the houses attributed to the Ellerbe firm from the 1920s until his death in an auto accident in 1957.

Despite his busy schedule, Crawford was active in the community, including the Masonic Lodge, Rotary, Rochester Golf and Country Club, Rochester Art Center and Calvary Episcopal Church. He was an active member and served as president of the Minnesota chapter of the American Institute of Architects in 1949–51.

In 1925 and 1926, he designed and had built his own Arts & Crafts–style cottage house at 514 8th Avenue SW. It was built on a challenging, steep double lot that Garfield Schwartz gave him as his commission for a project. The house is perched on the top (northern half) of the lot and looks different depending on whether it is approached from the north (small cottage) or south (larger Tudor). Harold doted on his colorful gardens extending below in the southern half of the lot. He lived there for the rest of his life, fifty-five years.

Harold's mother, Carrie, lived with them but never inhabited the lower-level apartment he designed for her. They rented it out for income. The first tenant in 1927 was an associate in the Division of Medicine, Phillip S. Hench, who won the Nobel Prize in 1950.

Between 1916 and 1965, Crawford designed seventy houses in southwest Rochester and twenty-three elsewhere, thirty commercial or agricultural buildings, fifteen government buildings, twelve schools, ten creameries, four medical buildings, four churches and four apartment buildings. I did not grow up in a Crawford house, but quite a few of my friends did. As a newly married medical student, I lived in the Crawford-designed duplex at 419 and 421 8th Avenue SW from 1975 to 1978, just a block from Crawford's own house. My personal favorites, each loaded with memories, are the Alfred Adson House (831 9th Avenue SW), Crawford's own house (514 8th Avenue SW), the old Public Library (now the Mitchell Student Center of Mayo Clinic Alix School of Medicine), Folwell School and the old post office (demolished).

Carrie died in 1936 at the age of seventy-six. That same year, May had a fall resulting in disabling fractures of her femur and pelvis from which she never fully recovered. To counterbalance all that sadness, in 1936 Harold met a destitute fifteen-year-old boy named Dale Corfits. He took him in as a foster son, and they remained close for life.

May never regained strength and died in 1945, leaving Harold alone in their house. Margaret was married by that time and living in California. She did provide Harold with two grandsons. Dale Corfits remained in Rochester and had three sons who were like grandsons to Harold. The Corfitses were Harold's local family late in life.

In retirement, Harold took up painting, almost exclusively in watercolor and primarily landscapes. His paintings are highly prized locally. Many of them are in the collections of Calvary Episcopal Church, the History Center of Olmsted County and the Rochester Art Center.

Margaret died in New York in 1970. Harold maintained correspondence with her sons as well as the Corfitses and his brother, Allen. He remained fairly healthy into his nineties but died somewhat unexpectedly on May 8, 1981, at the age of ninety-three. He is buried in Oakwood Cemetery, but his "memorial" is all over the region, especially in the distinctive houses of Southwest Rochester.[75]

ROCHESTER OLD SCHOOL BOYS AND GIRLS ASSOCIATION, 1916

The Rochester Old School Boys and Girls Association was created by Burt Eaton and others to facilitate a series of school reunions held at five-year intervals in Rochester between 1916 and 1941. Early in 1916, Stiles P. Jones and Dr. J.G. Cross, who lived in Minneapolis, proposed a reunion of Rochester graduates in Minneapolis. Rochester residents took over the idea and on October 15 and 16, 1916, held a reunion for the "Old Boys." Included were male graduates, aged forty-five to sixty, from Rochester High School, the Academy of Our Lady of Lourdes and Sanford Niles's private academy (which Will and Charlie Mayo attended). A contingent of eighty-three individuals, from the Twin Cities and beyond, chartered a private train for the event. They were met at the train station by the locals, paraded down Broadway to College (South 4th) St., back up Main Street (1st Avenue SW) to the old high school for a panoramic photo of the group (139 were in the photo out of 244 registered attendees), then off for automobile rides through town stopping at Schuster's Brewery for a beer before driving out to a reception at Mayowood hosted by "two score or more of our old girlfriends." A banquet was held that evening at the new high school (Coffman) building. Among the alumni attendees were U.S. Senators Porter J. McCumber (ND) and John B. Allen (WA); Frank B. Kellogg, elected to the U.S. Senate less than a month later, on November 7, 1916; and Catholic bishops Patrick R. Heffron of Winona and John J. Lawler of Lead, South Dakota. Speeches were given by Bishop Lawler, Frank Kellogg (who after a term in the Senate was U.S. ambassador to the United Kingdom, then U.S. secretary of state), Dr. Charlie Mayo and others. In the aftermath, the Rochester Old School Boys Association was incorporated by Burt Eaton and others, with Eaton as the perennial vice president.

The second reunion was held in October 1921. Women were included (adding "and Girls" to the title of the association) and the age limit was reduced to thirty-five, swelling the crowd to nine hundred. The banquet was held at the new Kahler (its first large banquet), and a dance was held at the new Armory, which was also headquarters for the meeting. The following day, visitors were treated to an automobile tour of the city followed by a reception at Dr. Will and Hattie Mayo's new house (the Foundation House). The records say nothing about the war, the Spanish flu or Prohibition but do include multiple expressions of confusion and dismay with the renaming of streets in 1918.

Rochester Old School Boys Association. Central panel of seven-panel panoramic group photograph. *From souvenir brochure* The Reunion at Rochester, Minnesota, *1916.*

Above: The Armory. *From History and Souvenir of Rochester, 1923, Mrs. J.R. Willis, Publisher.*

Left: Souvenir paper weights cast from remains of "Old Central" school bell. *Photo by Paul David Scanlon.*

The third reunion, on August 12–14, 1926, had 1,381 registered attendees. Knowing that no hall in town could host the dinner, the organizers rented a two-hundred-foot circus tent set up in Mayo Park. A dance was held at the Armory with 1,500 in attendance. A reception on the afternoon of the thirteenth was held at Dr. Henry and Daisy Plummer's new house and grounds. The banquet that evening was attended by 1,360, all fed promptly. Speeches followed, with Lieutenant Governor W.I. Nolan and Dr. Will Mayo as speakers. Dr. Charlie Mayo served as toastmaster. An additional special reception was held for the "Old Girls" at the Rochester Country Club.

The fourth reunion was held August 9–11, 1931, with more than 1,200 attendees. Miniature bells, cast from the fragments of the Central School bell (which was ruined in the Central School fire on September 1, 1910), were distributed as souvenirs. A dance was held on August 10 at the Armory.

The fifth reunion was held August 16–18, 1936. It was attended by about 1,500. The program included a band concert, a banquet in the circus tent with speeches and a dance at the Pla-Mor Ballroom.

The sixth and last reunion was August 17–19, 1941, after the deaths in 1939 of Drs. Will and Charlie Mayo. The reunion ball was held the evening of the eighteenth at the new Mayo Civic Auditorium. The banquet was on the nineteenth in the Mayo Civic Auditorium Arena. Congressman Allen J. Furlow was toastmaster, and speakers included Dr. Chuck Mayo, Harry Harwick and Bishop Lawler, who spoke at the first reunion. Why did it end? I found no record of explanation. The deaths of the Mayos? I suspect it was more likely the death of Burt Eaton later in 1941 and perhaps some of the other key organizers.[76]

College Apartments, 1918

Will and Hattie Mayo's "Red House" at 427 West College Street was a large Queen Anne–style house, completed in 1888. The Mayo brothers and their families lived side by side from the completion of Charlie and Edith's nearly identical "Yellow House" next door (419 West College Street) in 1894, until Charlie's family moved into Mayowood in 1911. Will and Hattie then initiated plans for their new home, now called the Foundation House, two blocks west up College Hill. When they moved out of the Red House, it was razed to make way for College Apartments, which opened in 1918. Ironically, the apartments were named after the street, which was renamed 4th Street SW the same year. Designed by Ellerbe & Associates and built by G. Schwartz & Co., they were designed to provide state-of-the-art "luxury rentals," primarily for young physicians. Facing 4th Street, they had fireproof construction with three stories plus basement and attic, containing fifty-eight rental units around a central courtyard for ventilation and light access. Decorated in Elizabethan Tudor style, the south-facing façade had a small central entry flanked by two full height gable-capped bays nearly filled with small paned casement windows. The lower levels were faced in red brick and the upper in stucco with half-timbering. The interiors were beautifully

College Apartment. *Postcard image.*

finished with quarter-sawn oak wainscoting and trim. They had all the modern amenities of the time, including central heat, electricity, including lights, and private bathrooms and kitchens (no air-conditioning yet). The south-facing apartments with bay windows were large and had fireplaces. The downtown location provided easy access to Mayo Clinic and affiliated hospitals. They were popular in their early years. In later years, dated fittings and facilities and lack of central air-conditioning decreased their appeal and they fell into disrepair. They were razed in 2007 to make way for a Mayo Clinic parking lot.[77]

LAKE ZUMBRO POWER DAM, 1919

In Rochester, electric power, water and sewer service are provided by Rochester Public Utilities, a publicly owned entity governed by a utility board, with four members appointed by the mayor for three-year terms, renewable once, plus one voting representative from city council. Public ownership of utilities (versus privately owned utility companies) is locally determined. It was the cause of many acrimonious debates in Rochester's history. W.W. Mayo and Mayor Julius Reiter were among the strong advocates for public ownership of utilities, who ultimately prevailed. Rates for electricity in Rochester are 9 percent below the statewide average and 12 percent below rates in Minneapolis, where electricity is provided by a publicly traded corporation. Water and sewage rates are comparable. Public utilities typically provide somewhat more reliable service as well.

Rochester's first electric plant in 1894 was a commercial entity owned by Western Electric Co. of Chicago. It was located on 3rd Street, just west of Broadway, and mainly provided electricity for city streetlights. Residences were still lit with kerosene lamps. It was destroyed by fire in 1915 and was replaced by a new city-owned main power generating facility built on North Broadway in 1916.

Meanwhile, interest in hydroelectric power grew, and in 1915, a bond referendum was approved for $650,000 for construction of the 440-foot-long by 60-foot-high Lake Zumbro Hydroelectric Generating Plant, commonly known as the Lake Zumbro power dam, fifteen miles north of Rochester, between Oronoco, Mazeppa and Zumbro Falls. It was designed by the famous civil engineer Colonel Hugh Lincoln Cooper (1865–1937), who was born in rural Houston County, seventy miles southeast of Rochester. After graduating from Rushford High School in 1883, he was self-taught as an engineer and worked as a bridge builder for the Chicago, Milwaukee and St. Paul Railroad for several years until he persuaded Horace Horton to hire him in Rochester. He worked his way up diligently as a bridge designer

Lake Zumbro power dam. *Postcard image.*

Turbines in Lake Zumbro power dam. *Postcard image.*

and engineer and was appointed superintendent and chief engineer when Horton founded Chicago Bridge & Iron Co. in 1889. Not long after that, Cooper left CB&I to pursue his new interest in hydroelectric engineering. Once again, he quickly worked his way up in the new field. He became renowned and operated an eponymous engineering firm on Park Avenue in New York City. He designed many major hydroelectric dams around the world, including Horseshoe Falls dam in Niagara, Ontario (1906); the Mississippi Lock and Dam No. 19 between Keokuk, Iowa, and Hamilton, Illinois (1910–13); the Aswan Dam in Egypt (1913–33); the Tennessee Valley Authority's Wilson Dam at Muscle Shoals, Alabama (1918–24); and the Dnieper River project in Ukraine, which was then part of the Soviet Union (1927–32). During World War I, he was a supervising engineer in the Army Corps of Engineers, decorated for his leadership in managing the military port in Bordeaux, France. He kept his relations with Rochester, of which his wife, Fanny Graves Cooper, was a native. He was a friend and correspondent of Dr. Will Mayo, who at one point skillfully advised Cooper in the medical care of his seriously ill daughter. When the Lake Zumbro dam was proposed in 1917, Cooper submitted the successful design proposal.[78]

The Lake Zumbro power dam was Cooper's only hydroelectric dam project in his home state. It has been listed on the National Register of Historic Places since 1991, largely because of Cooper's prominence. Built in 1917–19, the dam cost $300,000 above the original budget. It still produces two megawatts of power after 103 years in operation. That was thought sufficient to provide for all of Rochester's power needs in 1919. That estimate was naïve. With more available power, usage increased. An additional two-and-a-half-megawatt generator was installed at the North Broadway plant in 1925.

The lake created by the dam provides boating, fishing and other watersports to residents of Olmsted and Wabasha Counties. Olmsted is one of only four counties in Minnesota (with Mower, Pipestone and Rock) without a natural lake. It is 600 to 715 acres (0.9–1.1 square miles) in area, approximately 5 miles long and up to 43 feet deep near the dam.[79]

WOMEN'S SUFFRAGE, 1920

The struggle by women for the right to vote likely began before the birth of the nation in 1776. Some date the national women's suffrage movement as beginning at various dates between 1820 and 1850, particularly from the first women's rights convention, held in Seneca Falls, New York on July 19 and 20, 1848, six years before Rochester was settled. The Nineteenth Amendment to the U.S. Constitution was written by Susan B. Anthony and introduced in Congress in 1877. It was passed by Congress forty-two years later in 1919. Minnesota voters ratified it on September 8, 1919. It was ratified by the thirty-sixth state (Tennessee) and became law in 1920. The first national election in which all U.S. women were eligible to vote was in 1920, seventy-two years after the Seneca Falls convention. The League of Women Voters of Minnesota was organized in October 1919. Before the national amendment, states had the power to approve women's suffrage. On December 10, 1869, the Wyoming territorial legislature granted women the right to vote and to hold public office. When Wyoming became the forty-fourth state in 1890, it retained women's suffrage, the first state to do so, and became known as "The Equality State." New Jersey allowed women to vote until its state constitution outlawed it in 1844. Colorado (in 1893), Utah and Idaho (both in 1896) joined Wyoming by granting full or partial women's suffrage. Fifteen other states followed suit between 1910 and 1918, not including Minnesota.[80]

Sarah Burger Stearns (1836–1904) was among the earliest proponents for women's suffrage in Rochester. A native of Michigan, she had advocated for admission of women to the University of Michigan, a proposal that was

Left: Sarah Burger Stearns. *Right*: Marion Louisa Sloan. *Courtesy of the History Center of Olmsted County.*

eventually approved in 1869. She married in 1863 and moved to Rochester after the Civil War in 1866. Her husband, Colonel Ozora Stearns, an attorney, partnered with Charles Start. He served as mayor of Rochester in 1866–68 and U.S. senator briefly in 1871 before being appointed judge of the Eleventh Judicial District of Minnesota. Joseph A. Leonard, owner/editor of the *Rochester Post*, hired Sarah Stearns as a writer. Together, they created a powerful regional voice for women's suffrage through a series of articles and editorials.

In 1867, Stearns joined with Dr. Mary Jackman Colburn of Champlin and others to petition the Minnesota legislature to amend the state constitution by deleting the word *male* from details of voting rights. The proposed bill was defeated in committee by a single vote. A similar bill was defeated in 1869. In February 1870, the legislature passed a bill granting women the right to vote in Minnesota (House 33-13, Senate 21-9). The bill was vetoed by Governor Horace Austin on March 8, 1870.

In 1869, the Minnesota legislature passed a bill granting the right to vote to Black men but not to women. The Fifteenth Amendment to the

U.S. Constitution granted the same right to Black men nationally in 1870. Many women's suffragists felt betrayed, and it divided the national suffrage movement.

The Rochester Woman Suffrage Association (RWSA) was founded in 1869, the first such organization in the state. Sarah Stearns was a founding member and corresponding secretary of RWSA. She was active in Rochester until 1872, when she moved to Duluth. There, she organized the Duluth Woman Suffrage Circle and was the first woman to serve on the Duluth school board. In 1881, she and others founded the Minnesota Woman Suffrage Association (MWSA). Stearns served as the founding president. She went on to be vice president of the Minnesota Association for the Advancement of Women and of the National Woman Suffrage Association.[81]

In 1875, a majority of male voters in Minnesota approved an amendment to the state constitution to allow women to vote in elections pertaining to schools. In the years that followed, despite many efforts to expand women's voting rights, no further legislative progress was made in Minnesota. Charlotte Van Cleve was elected to the Minneapolis school board on April 5, 1876, to represent St. Anthony Village. The first woman elected to the Rochester school board was Amelia Hatfield Witherstine (1861–1949) in 1911, thirty-six years after the state amendment. She served on the school board until 1923, as president from 1914 to 1923.

The MWSA hosted the American Woman Suffrage Association national conference in 1885, bringing attention and leadership recognition to the MWSA and its members. The Olmsted County Woman Suffrage Association was founded in 1899.

Susan B. Anthony visited Rochester in 1877 to speak on Christmas Eve in Heaney Hall (the Opera House) on the third floor of the Heaney Block (northwest corner of Broadway and Zumbro Street (2nd Street SW)). Her speech was titled "Women Want Bread, Not the Ballot!" Other important Rochester speakers on suffrage included Frederick Douglass on February 21 and 22, 1868; Mary Livermore in 1873, 1874, 1878 and 1879; Frances Willard in 1880 and 1885; Dr. Katharine Bushnell in 1890; and Reverend Ida Hultin in 1899.

Eliza Tupper Wilkes was born in Maine and raised in Iowa. She served as minister of the Rochester Universalist Church briefly in 1869 and from 1870 to 1873. The church (along with the Congregational Church) was a focus of activity throughout the women's suffrage movement. Wilkes went on to establish eleven Universalist churches throughout the Midwest and West and was prominent in the national and international suffrage movement. She was honorary vice president of the National Women's Suffrage Association in 1884. She died in 1917 before passage of the Nineteenth Amendment.

Marion Louisa Sloan (1846–1942) was an early settler of Rochester who came with her family from Massachusetts to Rochester in 1856 at the age of ten. She was a leader of the suffrage movement in Minnesota, elected vice president of the Minnesota State Woman Suffrage Association in 1903–6. She was a regular diarist whose writings detail the evolution of the suffrage movement. She was one of the few early suffragists who lived long enough to vote in 1920, when Warren G. Harding was elected president.

Prohibition, 1920

The temperance movement to outlaw the sale of alcohol became popular at the beginning of the twentieth century. Many "dry" towns across the nation prohibited local sale of alcoholic beverages. The temperance movement was promoted by the Woman's Christian Temperance Union and many others, including medical organizations. Carry Nation was an outspoken advocate for national prohibition. She was renowned for verbal and sometimes physical attacks on saloons with a hatchet. Temperance gained momentum during World War I when it was thought that alcohol impeded the national war effort. Dr. Charlie Mayo spoke to the issue in 1917: "No one except the policeman sees more of the results of overindulgence in alcohol demonstrated in poverty, sickness, immorality, and crime than the physician. Medicine has reached a period when alcohol is rarely employed as a drug, being displaced by better remedies. Alcohol's only place now is in the arts and sciences. National prohibition would be welcomed by the medical profession."[82]

The Eighteenth Amendment to the U.S. Constitution prohibited the manufacture, sale, transportation, importation or exportation of intoxicating beverages in the United States and its territories. It was approved by Congress on December 18, 1917, and ratified by the last of the required number of states on January 16, 1919. The National Prohibition Act or Volstead Act, the law that implemented Prohibition, became effective on January 17, 1920. It was vetoed by President Woodrow Wilson but was overridden by both the House and Senate. Andrew Volstead, author of the bill, was born outside of Kenyon, Minnesota, in 1860. He lived in Granite Falls, Minnesota, when he was a U.S. representative. Interestingly, he was not a teetotaler. Kenyon

THE HOME OF *Schuster's* MALT AND HOP *Tonic* ——— Rochester, Minn. U.S.A.

Schuster's Brewery. *Postcard image.*

celebrated the one hundredth anniversary of the Volstead Act by having a special on drinks at the local municipal liquor store.[83]

The economic impact of Prohibition in Rochester was significant. In addition to the closure or transformation of all bars, saloons and restaurants, the Schuster Brewery went out of business. In 1910, Schuster's was Rochester's largest employer with fifty employees.[84] When Prohibition started, Schuster's attempted to adapt by increasing production of nonalcoholic malt tonic and switching from beer to "near beer "(less than 0.5 percent alcohol). Sales were not sufficient to maintain the large plant, so it closed in 1922. The plant was sold to Rochester Dairy Co. in 1925.[85]

Rumors exist regarding local speakeasies and other violations of Prohibition. They were virtually ubiquitous but are poorly documented. Much of the distilled spirits consumed in Southeast Minnesota apparently came from Canada by way of Michigan and Wisconsin, brought into the state and distributed by runners. John T. Lemmon served as Rochester mayor from 1925 to 1927 and from 1930 to 1931. He claimed a hard line for enforcement of Prohibition but was accused of purchasing alcohol illegally himself.[86]

Dr. Will Mayo was a strict teetotaler. Long after he died in 1939, alcohol was not served at his home, the Mayo Foundation House. However, thirty years later, when former president Lyndon Johnson joined Mayo Foundation's Board of Trustees in 1969, an exception was made for his evening glass of bourbon. Since that precedent was established, the Foundation House serves wine during some social events.

Before implementation, Prohibition was expected to reduce crime, improve health and protect young people. As it turned out, it dramatically increased crime, particularly organized crime, promoted disdain for the law and increased the corruption of law enforcement. It contributed to binge drinking and underage drinking. In the end, more than 65 percent of Minnesotans voted for repeal.[87] The Twenty-First Amendment was approved by Congress on February 20, 1933, and ratified by the necessary number of states on December 5, 1933. Its first clause states: "The eighteenth article of amendment to the Constitution of the United States is hereby repealed," thus ending national Prohibition.

Some counties and towns in other states remain dry to the present. In Minnesota, Chapter 23 of 1915, known as the "County Option Bill," authorized countywide prohibition of the sale of alcoholic beverages if approved by a simple majority of voters in a special election. In 1917, approximately half of Minnesota counties (mostly rural) were dry by vote. Olmsted was wet by vote. Once Prohibition ended, Minnesota reverted to the county option from 1915 (twenty-eight counties were dry in 1933, including Dodge, Fillmore, Freeborn and Faribault). In 1965, the legislature approved HF1400, and Governor Karl Rolvaag allowed it to become law, eliminating the authority of counties to restrict the sale of alcoholic beverages.[88] The so-called "Surly law" of 2011 eliminated the restriction on breweries from selling product on their premises. That spawned a new industry for brewpubs in the state. In 2017, Minnesota eliminated its century-old prohibition of liquor sales on Sundays. (It still bans the sale of vehicles on Sunday.) Minnesota is the last state in the nation that restricts grocery stores, gas stations and convenience stores from selling liquor, wine or beer stronger than 3.2 percent alcohol.

Mayo Clinic Institute of Experimental Medicine, 1922

The need for basic research by the evolving Mayo Clinic was not immediately apparent to Dr. Will Mayo. Drs. Henry Plummer and Louis Wilson argued that a research program was essential, "that it would broaden the horizon of staff members, and that it would prevent the practice of medicine from being limited to existing knowledge."[89]

Beginning in 1908, space was provided for animal surgical research in a barn at Dr. Wilson's house on 4th Street SW (for which he received a grant of $500 from the Mayo partnership) as well as a barn at the rear of St.

Mayo Clinic Institute for Experimental Medicine. From commemorative brochure for Twenty-Fifth Anniversary of the Mayo Foundation for Medical Education and Research, October 1940. *Used with permission of Mayo Foundation for Medical Education and Research. All rights reserved.*

Mary's Hospital that included two operating rooms and facilities for housing monkeys, dogs, rabbits, guinea pigs, rats, mice and pigeons. Dr. Frank C. Mann was appointed chief of the Division of Experimental Surgery in 1914. An attempt was made in the 1914 red brick Mayo Clinic building to accommodate animal research on the top floor, but the location was never satisfactory because of proximity to hotel guests looking down on the facility. In 1915, Dr. Charlie Mayo donated an eighty-acre tract of land at the top of Institute Road SW that was ideally suited for the purpose. The first animal care and housing facilities were built in 1916.

Beginning in 1922, construction of the Institute of Experimental Medicine (a name chosen by Dr. Will Mayo) commenced. The complex consisted of an eighty-six-by-thirty-five-foot three-story main laboratory building with basement and sub-basement, a three-story office building, a storage shed, various animal shelters, barns and a garage. At the time, it was considered a state-of-the-art animal research facility. When construction was nearly complete, on a windy evening, May 7, 1923, a fire burned all but the dog kennels and horse barns to the ground. The automatic sprinkler system was not yet connected to the water supply.[90] The cause of the suspicious fire was never determined. Rumors of arson by antivivisectionists circulated but were never proven.[91] It was decided to rebuild on the same foundations, which were undamaged by the fire. The facility finally opened in 1924 with nine researchers and twenty technicians. It gradually grew to provide a home for physiology, experimental surgery, anatomic and surgical pathology, bacteriology, biophysics, biochemistry, roentgenology and comparative anatomy. The laboratory-based work with streptomycin and Compound E (cortisone) were performed in labs at the institute. A strong Section of Physiology formed under leadership of Drs. Charles Code, Earl Wood and Edward Lambert, eventually forming the Mayo Aeromedical Unit.[92] The institute housed the first small centrifuge for animal experimentation by investigators of the Aero Medical Unit. A twenty-fifth anniversary document from 1949 noted that 1,400 publications (exclusive of abstracts) originated from the institute during that time.[93]

When the first portion of the Medical Sciences Building opened in 1941, some of the experimental surgery and animal research was transferred downtown. It housed, in an adjacent structure, the human centrifuge that was central to the acceleration work of the Aero Medical Unit. A larger twenty-thousand-square-foot addition to Medical Sciences was built around the centrifuge in 1951, allowing other sections to transfer downtown. These included Sections of Anatomy, Biochemical Research, Biophysics, Electroencephalography, Engineering, Pathologic Anatomy, Physiology, Surgical Research, X-ray storage and a surgical specimen library, as well as animal care facilities and radioisotope handling facilities. The institute continued to support research in infectious diseases, experimentation with large animals and large colonies of small animals, as well as breeding, receiving and holding of animals for experimental work. In 1955, the complex was renamed Institute Hills Farm as an acknowledgement of its changed function.[94] Medical Sciences remained the primary center for animal-based research until the Murry and Léonie Guggenheim Building was dedicated on October 18, 1974. The Guggenheim space was doubled with a vertical addition in 1987. Additional research lab space was added with the construction of the ten-story Vincent Stabile Building, dedicated in 2006 and 2007.

BELVA SNODGRASS, 1922

Belva Snodgrass was born in Indianapolis on October 20, 1890. She started her career in Rochester in 1922. Beginning as a teacher, she rose quickly through the ranks as dean of students, director of student accounting, fifteen years as principal of Rochester High School and then

Belva Snodgrass. *Courtesy of the History Center of Olmsted County.*

principal of the junior high school from 1940 until retiring in 1956 after thirty-four years. She was beloved by some as a creative and supportive administrator but was also a strict disciplinarian. She is credited with starting the Girl Scouts in Rochester in 1927.

Snodgrass was a creative problem solver. It is reported that "during the 1930s, when a wave of Halloween vandalism struck the city, she used her position as principal of Rochester High School to organize yearly Halloween parties at the high school [with required attendance]. She also brokered a deal with local businesses and the students: if the vandalism stopped, the Soldiers Memorial Field football field would get lights." In 1936, the lights went up.

In other testimonials, it was noted that "she was known for persuading dropouts to return to school and bought graduation suits for boys whose families couldn't afford them."

In 1954, she became the first woman to be named to the Police Civil Service Commission. After her retirement from the district in 1956, she served as director of training and education at Kahler Corp, and she was appointed to the Rochester Public Utilities Board, the first woman to serve in that role.

In 1971, on Snodgrass's eighty-first birthday, Mayor Dewey Day declared Belva Snodgrass Day. She was joined by over three hundred former students at a celebration party.[95]

In 1980, when the school board was seeking a name for a new middle school, Belva Snodgrass was considered but drew negative responses. "Let them have their fun," said Snodgrass, "There's always been wise-cracking about my name." She also said, "No child wants to attend a school named Snodgrass." The school board settled on Willow Creek.[96] In 1975, she returned to her hometown of Indianapolis, where she died on May 1, 1983, at the age of ninety-two.[97]

F.E. WILLIAMS'S LEGACY, 1927

Frank E. Williams, better known as F.E. Williams, was a quiet businessman. He owned and managed a farm implement store that he inherited from his better-known father, Colonel D.H. Williams, a Civil War hero. F.E. cared about children's safety and did something to ensure it. He left his real estate holdings to the city's Department of Parks and Recreation, the income to be used for children's playground equipment. That legacy is still alive ninety years later in the F.E. Williams Trust.

His father, Colonel Dennis Hogan Williams, was born in Ohio in 1832. He served in the Forty-Third Ohio Infantry during the Civil War and was promoted from first lieutenant to colonel. He came to Rochester with his wife and two children in 1868 and engaged in the farm implement business, first in partnership with J. Franklin Van Dooser, then alone. He served one term as alderman and three one-year terms as mayor of Rochester (1873–75 and 1878–79). He also served on the school board from 1886 to 1896. He died in 1911 and is buried in Oakwood Cemetery with his wife and family.[98]

Frank was born in Ohio on June 23, 1860, the second of four children. He was seven years old when the family moved to Rochester. He joined his father in the farm implement business, located on Main Street (1st Avenue SW) and

F.E. Williams Building in 1983. *Courtesy of the Rochester Post Bulletin.*

F.E. Williams's (recently demolished) house on Fifth Street SW. *Postcard image.*

3rd Street. He married Frances "Fanny" Johndro in 1880. She died in 1890 shortly after giving birth to their only child, a daughter named Frances. She, in turn, developed tuberculosis at the age of fifteen and died at the age of nineteen in 1910. He mourned their deaths deeply. He sold his business in 1912 but retained his real estate and the income from it. It was noted that he loved parks and frequently visited Soldiers Field and Mayo Park, both of which are close to his home and his business.

He frequently played checkers in the evening with his friend William Klee at Klee's grocery store on 5th Street SW. One evening as they were playing, they heard the screech of a car stopping in front of the store. They looked to see that the car had just missed hitting a child playing in the street—fortunately the child was unharmed. Williams is quoted as saying: "Rochester should have more playgrounds, so children need not play in the streets." A friend asked, "Why don't you do something about it? You have property." Williams responded, "I will." On October 18, 1927, Williams executed his will in which he left his property to the City of Rochester "for the use of the Park Board...for the acquiring of, or for the support of, or for the maintenance of...playgrounds for children under the age of 15 years."

When Williams died on May 18, 1932, at the age of seventy-one, his bequest included five-eighths interest in his farm implement building at the southeast corner of 1st Avenue and 3rd Street SW, which still exists. It was the home to Bilotti's Pizza for sixty years (1955–2015) and currently houses the

Half Barrel Bar & Restaurant as well as John Kruesel's General Merchandise. The bequest also included a house (later an apartment building) at 506 5th Street SW and a house at 109 4th Street SW. The three properties were valued at $57,000. The city sold the two residential properties in exchange for the additional three-eighths interest in the commercial building. In the ninety years since his death, the trust has yielded over $500,000 expended for its stated purpose. It has provided playground equipment throughout the city. In 1984, when the cost of maintaining the old building became a disadvantage, the city sold the commercial building. A vacant adjacent property was sold in 2010 for the 318 Commons student housing facility for University of Minnesota–Rochester. Proceeds of those sales were added to the trust account. The F.E. Williams Trust now has a principal value over $600,000. Its funds are used by the Department of Parks and Recreation for purposes in keeping with the terms of the bequest.[99]

Libby's (Reid-Murdoch, Monarch, then Libby, McNeill & Libby, then Seneca Foods), 1929

The Monarch Foods vegetable canning facility was at the southwest corner of the intersection of 3rd Avenue SE and "The Beltline" (12th Street or U.S. Highway 14). It was built by Reid, Murdoch & Co. of Chicago as their principal pea and corn production facility. It opened for business on June 10, 1929. The event coincided with the Diamond Jubilee of Rochester and consisted of a parade of three hundred representatives of Reid, Murdoch & Co., who came from Chicago on two chartered trains. Miss America Lois Delander of Joliet, Illinois, and an eighty-piece high school band were also included. The group paraded from the train station to the new factory. Reid-Murdoch's Ford Tri-motor aircraft, stocked with Monarch Food products, flew over the city and gave free rides to citizens from the airport (just a few blocks from the factory). A celebration and dance were held at the factory in the evening.

The building was initially 127 by 300 feet, set on an 11-acre plot wedged against the Chicago & Great Western tracks. It grew to 100,000 square feet (2,087,750 cubic feet). The daily capacity initially exceeded 480,000 cans of peas or corn. The product was grown on contract by initially 30, up to 140 farms, using 4,000 acres for peas and 7,000 acres for corn (23,700 acres in later years). An annual three- to four-week pea season in June and five-week

Monarch Foods (Reid-Murdoch, Monarch, then Libby, McNeill & Libby, then Seneca Foods). *Postcard image.*

corn season in August and September yielded 24 up to 180 million cans of vegetables (increasing over the years) and employed up to 1,200–1,300 part-time seasonal workers in two shifts (decreasing to 300 in later years with automation). Production always emphasized freshness, with as little as one to two hours from field to can. The facility also canned lima beans, kidney beans, carrots and various combinations of mixed vegetables.

The plant was bought by Libby, McNeill & Libby in 1948 and was commonly known as Libby's during my youth. It was a default employer for many high school students during the summer. Working conditions were often hot in the un-air-conditioned plant but otherwise not too unpleasant, as manual labor jobs go (i.e., easier than farm work). My brother worked there two summers, as did many friends.

S.S. Pierce Co. Inc. of Dundee, New York, bought Libby's canned vegetables division in 1982 and managed it under their Seneca Foods brand until closing in 2018. In 2019, Olmsted County bought the building and eleven-acre grounds for $5.6 million. The building was demolished in 2021 and the property regraded, preserving the iconic ear of corn water tower, which was repaired and repainted, also in 2021. Seneca continues to employ about 160 people to process and distribute frozen vegetables at its frozen food facility farther south on 3rd Avenue SE.[100]

The story of the iconic 149-foot-tall ear of corn or "The Corn Cob" water tower, in use since 1931, is detailed elsewhere.[101]

LUCY WILDER AND DOROTHY DAY, 1933

Lucy Elizabeth Beeler was born in Hamilton, Ohio, on May 15, 1889, and married Dr. Russell Wilder on March 18, 1911. They spent a year in Vienna in 1914 and otherwise lived in Chicago before moving to Rochester in 1919. Russell was an endocrinologist and researcher specializing in diabetes. He worked at Mayo Clinic from 1919 to 1929 and 1931 to 1950. Like many spouses of Mayo physicians, Lucy longed for the amenities of a larger city. In 1933, she bought the bookstore at 113 1st Avenue SW and renamed it "The Bookstore of Lucy Wilder."

Lucy managed the store like a European salon, hosting intellectual conversations for all sorts of customers. She succeeded in drawing in an international clientele that included not only physicians and Mayo Clinic visitors but also a broad variety of intellectuals from all over the map. She served tea and wine in the afternoon to promote conversation, usually starting with books but branching to other topics, including politics. Lucy Wilder was a very liberal protofeminist who smoked a pipe and had an opinion about nearly everything. She was well liked in the community.

The manager of the store, whose employment was continued by Wilder, was Mary Dorothy "Dodie" Day (1898–1969). They became close friends. So close, in fact, that in 1947, Lucy gave Day the store as a Christmas gift.

A different Dorothy Day (1897–1980), for whom Dorothy Day House is named, was a Chicago Catholic anarchist human rights activist. She was a contemporary of Wilder and Day, so it is possible they were acquainted and likely that they knew of her and her activism.

The bookstore had a mascot, a Great Dane named Thor. He stationed himself outside the door, drank from the public fountain down the street and delivered the day's receipts to the bank every afternoon in a pouch.

In 1936, Lucy published *The Mayo Clinic*, a brief (eighty-two pages) history of Mayo Clinic, preceding Helen Clapesattle's *The Doctors Mayo* by five years. It went through at least four revisions over the years.

The bookstore had friendly competition around the corner at Adams' Book & Art Shop in the Massey Building at 16 2nd Street SW. It was founded in 1901 and operated in the same location for sixty-four years until it was sold to Farnham's Stationery, of Minneapolis, in 1965. It operated as Farnham-Adams for less than two years until it closed.

Russell retired as chair of the Department of Medicine of Mayo Foundation in 1950. The Wilders then moved to Washington, where Russell was appointed the founding director of the new National Institute of

Lucy Wilder and Dorothy Day graves. *Photo by Paul David Scanlon.*

Arthritis and Metabolic Diseases. He left that position in 1953 because of health problems, and they returned to Rochester. Day continued to own and manage the store until selling it in 1965. It went through a series of owners until closing in 1975.

Russell died on December 16, 1959, at which point Lucy invited Dorothy to move into the Wilders' house at 705 8th Avenue SW. Lucy died at St. Mary's Hospital on July 13, 1968. Dorothy died on November 25, 1969. Russell, Lucy and Dorothy are buried together, in that order, in Oakwood Cemetery.[102]

RICHARD J. DORER, 1938

The Whitewater, Root and Zumbro Rivers were pristine in their natural state, but less than a century after the arrival of the first white settlers, they were all in poor condition. The Whitewater Valley, particularly, was so badly eroded by the 1930s that it became prone to frequent flooding. Several towns in the valley, Beaver and Whitewater Falls, became uninhabitable because of flooding and silting and are now ghost towns. Richard J. Dorer began working for the Minnesota Department of Conservation in 1938, the worst year in history for flooding by the Whitewater River. He proposed and gained approval for the purchase of thirty-eight thousand acres (fifty-nine square miles) along the Whitewater River for a wildlife area that eventually became Whitewater State Park and State Forest. Several state agencies in partnership replanted the valleys and slopes, contoured the upland fields

Richard J. Dorer's grave marker in Beaver Cemetery. *Photo by Paul David Scanlon.*

and built diversion dams at the tops of gullies. Dorer designed a system of dikes to control runoff in what are now called the Richard J. Dorer Pools.[103]

Dorer was visionary and instrumental in restoring the bluff country, rivers and streams elsewhere in southeast Minnesota, leading the state to acquire and restore the land that became the Richard J. Dorer Memorial Hardwood State Forest, the largest state forest in Minnesota (1,016,227 acres or 1,588 square miles in noncontiguous parcels), right here in Southeast Minnesota.

In 1951 the Izaak Walton League Minnesota Division helped launch a campaign to "Save Our Wetlands" which were rapidly disappearing due to farming drainage. Led by IKE leader Richard J. Dorer, who was a manager in the Minnesota Department of Conservation, the campaign developed into a major program to buy wetlands and other threatened habitat. Today, the program has become a network of over 1,440 public wildlife areas with 1.4 million acres of habitat, from prairies and wetlands to forests and swamps, for Minnesota's wildlife species.[104]

Richard Jacob Dorer was born on December 18, 1889, in Belmont County, Ohio. He died in Whitewater Township, Winona County on October 13, 1973, and is buried in Beaver Cemetery, east of Plainview in the Whitewater Valley. His grave is marked with a wooden sign with a metal cutout in the shape of Minnesota incised in block print, all capitals, as follows:

··STEWARDSHIP··
YOUR CREATOR
HAS FILLED THE EARTH
WITH ALL THINGS NECESSARY
TO SUSTAIN YOU
AND HAS FOUND THEM
TO BE GOOD.
WHILE YOU DWELL
AMONG THE MORTALS
YOU MAY PARTAKE
THEROF.
USE THEM WISELY
AND JUDICIOUSLY.
GUARD THEM CLOSELY.
SQUANDER THEM NOT.
IF YOU ARE UNTRUE
TO THE SACRED TRUST
MANKIND
SHALL NOT BE
PERPETUATED
BUT SHALL BANISH
ITSELF
FROM THE EARTH.
RICHARD J. DORER

BORN DEC. 18, 1889, BELMONT COUNTY,
OHIO, THE THIRD CHILD OF CARL AND JULIA
DORER. FATHER, IMMIGRANT FROM GERMANY. MOTHER,
SIMPLE PERSON OF GREAT GOODNESS AND
SPIRITUALITY.
ATTENDED GRADE AND HIGH SCHOOL IN
BELLAIRE, RECEIVED HIGHER EDUATION AT
THE U.S. MILITARY ACADEMY AT WEST POINT N.Y.
SERVED AS CAPTAIN WITH THE 147TH
FIELD ARTILLERY BATTERY A, 32ND DIVISION
WISCONSIN MICHIGAN. RECEIVED THE PURPLE
HEART, THE FRENCH CROIX DE GUERRE—TWICE
AND WAS CITED FOR THE DISTINGUISHED
SERVICE CROSS DURING W.W.I.
HE IS REGARDED AS THE FATHER OF THE
SAVE THE WETLANDS MOVEMENT, THE INSTIGATOR
OF THE MINNESOTA MEMORIAL HARDWOOD
FOREST AND THE OUTSTANDING SPOKESMAN FOR
GOOD CONSERVATION PRACTICES. HE RECEIVED
THE NASH CONSERVATION AWARD AND THE
VALLEY FORGE FOUNDATION MEDAL.
HE WAS LAID TO REST OCT. 13, 1973.

ROCHESTER AIRPORT (RST/LOBB FIELD) DURING WORLD WAR II, 1941

The airfield in southeast Rochester, later called Lobb Field, was the third field to host aircraft for landings and takeoffs in Rochester. It was in southeast Rochester, what is now the Meadow Park neighborhood, between 4th and 11th Avenues SE and between 13th and 20th Streets SE. It was preceded from 1912 to 1928 by Graham Field extending south from the county fairgrounds across what is now 16th Street SE between 1st and 2nd Avenues SE. From June to November 1928, an airfield was provided by Rochester Air Ways at 2nd Street and 23rd Avenue SW. What became Lobb Field was initially 120 acres, owned and operated by Rochester Airport Company, a subsidiary of Mayo Properties Association. The runways were grass, initially. The airport was managed by Albert J. Lobb, a Mayo Clinic administrator. It was first used on October 28, 1928, and was dedicated on June 11, 1929. Air mail service was established on March 8, 1930. In the years before World War II, it became increasingly busy, and the aircraft became larger, heavier and faster. Northwest Airlines served ten thousand passengers in Rochester in 1939. NWA helped fund a new passenger terminal and space for radio guidance equipment. Before the United States entered the war, Mayo Properties Association funded improved ground control equipment and an expansion of the airport to 370 acres. Its four runways were extended to 3,400 long by 150 feet wide and were paved (see below). The airport was rededicated on August 4, 1940. A weather bureau was installed in 1942, and a radio control tower was built and equipped with the latest technology in 1943.

The terms of the Lend-Lease Act of 1941 called for the United States to lend military supplies and other strategic materials to embattled allies, first Great Britain and subsequently France, China and the Soviet Union. We provided aircraft to the Soviet Union for air combat over the eastern front against Germany. In September 1943, the Eleventh Ferrying Service Detachment, U.S. Air Transport Command, was stationed at Lobb Field to

In an undated memoir, Albert Lobb described a conversation with Dr. Will near the end of his life:

In the summer of 1939, Dr. William J Mayo was ill at home....[He] said to me, "What does the airport really need?" I told him about the runways that were needed. He replied, "Why don't you have them built?" [WJM then discussed with members of the board of Mayo Properties Association to assure approval.] I believe no other privately owned airport was so useful to the government during that period. For example, airplanes built in Buffalo, New York, were flown in great numbers to the Rochester Airport, where pilots were stationed to continue the flights to points in western Canada, where Russian pilots were waiting to fly the airplanes to Russia, our ally at that time....I was amazed to hear the remark: "You know, those Russian pilots who ferry the planes from Canada to Russia are women." The American pilots to whom I talked could not say enough about how those girls did their jobs.[105]

help ferry military aircraft to the Soviet Union via Canada for what turned out to be the final two years of the war. The reasons Rochester was used included its convenient location, its newly equipped radio control tower and weather station, the fact that it was less busy than Minneapolis and St. Paul airports, its newly paved runways and excellent snow removal.

The aircraft provided were mostly Bell P-39 Airacobra fighter planes and the next generation Bell P-63 Kingcobras. Of the 9,584 P-39s built during World War II, 4,773 were sent to the Soviet Union. Of the 3,303 P-63s built, virtually all went to the Soviets. The aircraft were ferried by the Air Transport Command pilots, some of whom were women of the WASP (Women Airforce Service Pilots) program. From the Bell factory in Niagara Falls, New York, aircraft were flown through a series of stops, including Rochester, refueling and changing pilots as needed. They flew on via North Dakota into western Canada, where Soviet pilots accepted the planes and flew via the Aleutian Islands and on to Siberia. After the first few months of the ferrying service, Gopher Aviation opened in July 1944 to service and repair aircraft. It also provided an air ambulance service, a flight school and a charter airline. Repair services were comprehensive, up to and including rebuilding 2,800-horsepower eighteen-cylinder radial engines for commercial airliners. After the war, Gopher Aviation became the largest aircraft repair facility between Chicago and California.[106]

With the combination of ferried fighter planes, commercial aviation, private aviation and flights by the "Gee-Whiz" (testing equipment for the Mayo Section of Physiology's Aero Medical Unit), it is

The Bell P-39 Airacobra was not popular among U.S. or British fighter pilots, but the Soviet aces loved it and had the highest "kill" rates of any Allied aircraft. Its 1,710-cubic-inch-displacement 2,300-horsepower Allison V12 engine performed well at lower altitudes, but it had only a single-stage, single-speed supercharger that limited high-altitude performance, giving it a practical ceiling between fifteen and twenty-five thousand feet. Soviet pilots flew primarily ground support, so they rarely operated at higher altitudes. Also, the P-39 was both more maneuverable and more unstable than any German aircraft. For inexperienced pilots that was a liability, but with experience and skill, that became an asset. Lastly, its giant thirty-seven-millimeter fuselage cannon was capable of making a kill with a single shot. It had four wing-mounted .50-caliber machine guns as well.

estimated that for each of the last two years of the war, ten thousand takeoffs or landings occurred per year at the Rochester airport, often as frequently as every three to four minutes. On at least one occasion, an incoming squadron of fifteen P-39s landed in rapid sequence. Rochester was also a center for training of glider pilots for the war effort.

It is said that women pilots who stayed overnight were quartered at Hilltop Guest House (now Hilltop House), built for Dr. J.T. Asbury in 1928 at 1735 3rd Avenue NW, at the east end of Assisi Heights, beyond the Wilson House and Indian Heights Park overlooking Silver Lake.[107]

DRS. ALDRICH AND SPOCK, 1944

The Rochester Epidemiology Project has made Olmsted County renowned internationally as the best-studied population in the world (see pages 149–50), but citizens of Rochester are mostly unaware of that aspect of their medical fame. Likewise, it can be argued that modern childrearing was born in Rochester, at least in part, and that is also largely unknown in Rochester. The only reminder of this history is the name of the Aldrich School, a private nonprofit nursery school in northwest Rochester. Who were Drs. Aldrich and Spock?

Charles Anderson "Andy" Aldrich was born in Plymouth, Massachusetts, on March 4, 1888. He attended Northwestern University for both college (where he was captain of the basketball team) and medical school (MD, 1915). After internship, he became a partner in a general medical practice at Evanston Hospital, where he developed an interest in pediatrics. In 1921, he took a year of advanced training in pediatrics in New York and Boston, then returned to Evanston and Chicago to practice pediatrics exclusively. He developed some innovative practices in preventive pediatrics along with expertise in pediatric kidney diseases. In addition to his academic publications, he published three popular books on child development and rearing. The best known, *Babies Are Human Beings* (1938), described normal development of an infant during its first year with practical "do's and don'ts" of early childrearing. It went through nineteen printings in under eight years. Aldrich played important roles in founding the American Academy of Pediatrics and the American Board of Pediatrics and served as editor of or on the editorial boards of several prominent pediatrics journals. He advanced to full professor of pediatrics at Northwestern in 1941. In that

Left: Dr. Charles Anderson "Andy" Aldrich. *Right*: Dr. Benjamin Spock. *Used with permission of Mayo Foundation for Medical Education and Research.*

year, Dr. Joseph Brennemann retired as chief of staff at Children's Memorial Hospital in Chicago. Aldrich was offered and accepted the position, and he hoped to develop a pediatric center for preventive care. His hope did not materialize in Chicago.

Three years later, in 1944, Mayo Foundation created the Rochester Child Health Project (RCHP, later the Rochester Child Health Institute or RCHI) to study child health in the community under the leadership of Dr. Henry F. Helmholz, head of the Section of Pediatrics. Helmholz recruited Aldrich as director, giving him the opportunity for preventive care that he had hoped to develop in Chicago. He accepted. The project was planned as a citywide (population thirty-three thousand) birth-to-adulthood longitudinal intervention study to continue for at least twenty years. Using pediatricians, psychologists and a nutritionist in conjunction with the city and county departments of health and the school nurses, Aldrich developed a program of preventive childcare for the entire community of Rochester. It drew international attention, including from the World Health Organization. Aldrich believed a nursery school to be an essential part of childcare in the community. His philosophy was to provide a safe, comfortable environment where children can explore and create at their own pace. He joined forces with a voluntary women's group to establish the Rochester Demonstration Nursery School under the direction of RCHP staff. It was later renamed the Aldrich Memorial Nursery School and eventually shortened to the Aldrich School, its current name. The current school is the direct descendant of the original and seeks to preserve its philosophy and practices.

Benjamin Spock was the author of the bestseller *The Common Sense Book of Baby and Child Care* (circa 1946, fifty million copies sold in fifty-two years, translated into thirty-nine languages, still in print as *Dr. Spock's Baby and Child Care*, 10th edition) and became the best-known pediatrician of several generations, His ideas about child rearing created modern parenting and influenced generations of parents and children. The name of *Star Trek's* Mr. Spock was unrelated.

Spock was born in New Haven, Connecticut, on May 2, 1903. He was educated at Yale (BA, plus a gold medal for rowing in the 1924 Paris Olympics) and Columbia (MD, 1929) Universities. His early career was mostly at Cornell Medical Center in New York. In 1944–46, he served as lieutenant commander in the medical corps of the U.S. Naval Reserve. Aldrich recruited Spock to Rochester in January 1947. He was appointed the second consultant in the Section on Psychiatry, the first child psychiatrist. Half of his time was assigned to RCHP, the other half to the teaching and practice of clinical child psychiatry. In 1949, Spock wrote the five-year summary of the RCHP. He described it thus: "A focal point which draws together agencies, individuals, and points of view in the field of child health, and then tries to bring them to bear on the children through available activities." Spock later said, "To be able to supervise the health care of an entire city was very unique."

In 1948, Aldrich received the Lasker Award ("America's Nobel") from the National Committee for Mental Hygiene for "outstanding contributions to the education of physicians in the psychological aspect of the practice of medicine." Sadly, in 1949, he developed pancreatic cancer and died within six months on October 6. After his death, institutional priorities changed, and the RCHP was defunded and discontinued in 1951. Spock said of the RCHP, "It helped to start a trend" toward the establishment of child development programs elsewhere. Spock left Mayo Clinic and went to the University of Pittsburgh (1951–55), then Case Western Reserve University (1955–67). In his "retirement years," Spock became a liberal antiwar political activist who ran for president of the United States as the People's Party nominee in 1972 (78,756 votes out of 76 million, Nixon won with

46.7 million votes). Spock remained an outspoken national voice of the political left, much like Senator Bernie Sanders. He died in San Diego on March 15, 1998, at the age of ninety-four.[108]

STREPTOMYCIN: WILLIAM FELDMAN AND H. CORWIN HINSHAW AND THE MISSED NOBEL PRIZE, 1945

Tuberculosis (TB) has been the greatest and most consistent infectious killer throughout human history. Also called "The White Plague" and "Captain of the Men of Death," it is estimated that TB killed about a quarter of the adult population of Europe in the nineteenth century, as well as many children and young adults. Even today, with effective treatment available, about 25 percent of humanity carries latent TB infection, and over one million people die of the disease annually.

The bacteria that cause TB are very resistant to most conventional antibacterial antibiotics. In the early antibiotic era, that fact was quickly apparent as trials with sulfanilamide, sulfapyridine, sulfathiazole and sulfamerazine all failed to affect the bacteria or the course of disease.

William Feldman was a Scottish immigrant and veterinarian researcher. He joined the Division of Experimental Medicine at Mayo Clinic as an instructor in comparative pathology in 1927. Corwin Hinshaw began his career with a doctorate in zoology in 1927 and developed an interest in parasitology. He then received a medical degree in 1933 from the University of Pennsylvania and then became a fellow in medicine at Mayo Clinic. Although he was initially interested in gastroenterology, he accepted a position in thoracic diseases (pulmonary medicine) and concentrated his research interest in the treatment of pneumonia. The two joined forces to work on developing treatments for tuberculosis. They developed a strict laboratory methodology for testing the effectiveness of treatments for tuberculosis using a virulent strain of TB in a sensitive animal, the guinea pig. In 1941, they reported an equivocal result with a sulfone compound called Promin (which was subsequently found to be more effective in treating leprosy). They searched carefully for a newer and better agent.

Before Selman Waksman identified streptomycin in 1943 at Rutgers University in New Jersey, Feldman requested a visit to Waksman's lab to discuss antibiotic discovery and trials. Feldman visited on November 16, 1943. It is not clear whether Waksman's subsequent studies of streptomycin with *Mycobacterium tuberculosis* (MTB) were prompted by Feldman's visit. In

Left: Dr. H. Corwin Hinshaw. *Right*: Dr. William H. Feldman. *Used with permission of Mayo Foundation for Medical Education and Research.*

January 1944, Waksman reported on streptomycin, including its effect on MTB in cultures. On March 1, Waksman wrote to Feldman to inquire whether he was prepared to test streptomycin on guinea pigs. He provided them with a supply sufficient for preliminary testing in four guinea pigs. It was well tolerated and seemed to be effective in a brief trial. With more streptomycin provided by Merck and Company, they began testing a larger group of guinea pigs in August 1944 and reported their preliminary results in December 1944 and their larger study in 1945. Streptomycin appeared to have a dramatic effect.

Feldman and Hinshaw then performed clinical trials of streptomycin, mainly with patients at the Mineral Springs Sanitorium in Cannon Falls, Minnesota. The first was a twenty-one-year-old woman with end-stage pulmonary TB treated from November 20, 1944, to April 7, 1945. She was apparently cured and subsequently married and had three children and no sign of recurrent or relapsed disease. They treated thirty-three more patients by September 1945. They reported their preliminary results in treating patients in the *Proceedings of the Staff Meetings of the Mayo Clinic* in 1945 and a summary of their first 100 cases in the *Journal of the American Medical Association* (*JAMA*) in 1946. Their results were dramatic, but they worded their reports cautiously so as not to raise hopes unreasonably in the early stages of treatment. The problem of drug resistance quickly became apparent, so the almost simultaneous development of para-amino-salicylic acid (PAS), another effective agent, was fortunate, and it was quickly added to treatment protocols. Later, even more effective drugs, such as isoniazid, ethambutol and rifampin, were added. Tuberculosis remains a major killer, particularly with the emergence of multidrug resistant strains of MTB; however, the antibiotic era has made the disease much more readily treatable.

Waksman and his colleagues at Rutgers University had an acrimonious battle over the distribution of royalties from the sale of streptomycin, which was settled in 1950. He received a solo Nobel Prize in Physiology or Medicine in 1952 for "your ingenious, systematic and successful studies of the soil microbes that have led to the discovery of streptomycin." Since then, there has been much commentary regarding the lack of acknowledgement of his co-developers both by Waksman and by the Nobel Committee. Many feel that Feldman and Hinshaw deserved more recognition than they received, that they should have received the Nobel Prize with Waksman.[109]

III

MODERN TIMES (1945–PRESENT)

Mayor Claude H. "Bony" McQuillan, 1947

Claude Henry McQuillan was born on June 21, 1888, in Rochester, Minnesota, to John Henry McQuillan (twenty-eight) and Emma Reiser McQuillan (twenty). In his youth, he was a professional football player for the Green Bay Packers (pre-NFL), a professional light heavyweight boxer who won twenty-nine of thirty bouts and a professional baseball player, a catcher. He was nicknamed "Bony" during his football years. Harry Harwick, in his autobiography, wrote: "While at Winona High School, from which I graduated in 1906, I vividly remember playing both football and baseball against a powerful and aggressive young man from Rochester, far better than I at both sports: Claude H. McQuillan, now Mayor of Rochester."[110]

Mayor Claude H. "Bony" McQuillan. *Courtesy of the History Center of Olmsted County.*

McQuillan had a diverse career. In addition to coaching and refereeing in all of his sports, he owned and operated a roller rink and ice rink, auctioned real estate, invented a take-up mechanism for movie film, constructed and installed air conditioners and worked in advertising at the *Post Bulletin*, eventually serving as advertising manager.

McQuillan married Marian Elizabeth Lampman (born on March 6, 1909) on June 29, 1932, in Crown Point, Indiana. McQuillan served

Claude H. "Bony" McQuillan
during his baseball career.
*Courtesy of the History Center of
Olmsted County.*

as alderman for the Third Ward from 1944 to 1947. In March 1947, he defeated incumbent mayor Paul Grassle (3,003 to 2,067) to be elected to the first of two two-year terms. After being reelected in 1949, he did not run for reelection in 1951. He sat out for two years, after which he was reelected again in 1953 to the first of three more two-year terms. As mayor, McQuillan was popular, never losing in seven bids for city office.

He was aggressive but egalitarian in office, blocking fluoridation of the drinking water supply, supporting the placement of Rochester Art Center in Mayo Park, advocating annexation of newly developed residential neighborhoods, rather than allowing independent incorporation of suburbs, leading the policy changes needed for construction of the new airport and supporting local sports in many ways. In 1953, a new high school was proposed to be built in Soldiers Field Park. The American Legion post opposed the location. The city council voted to transfer a portion of Soldiers Field to the school district, but McQuillan vetoed the resolution. The council overrode his veto, but McQuillan refused to sign the deed to transfer title for the land. The dispute was settled in district court where Judge Arnold Hatfield affirmed McQuillan's veto. The current northwest location of John Marshall High School was the result. (See separate story regarding McQuillan's pre–civil rights era stand against exclusion and racist language.[111])

McQuillan died, likely due to a sudden cardiac arrest, while still in office on November 16, 1957, in Rochester at the age of sixty-nine. He is buried in Oakwood Cemetery beside his wife.[112] McQuillan Field, on Marion Road SE, is named in his honor.

Marian McQuillan served as her husband's secretary while he was mayor and continued in that role for three succeeding mayors after him: Adolph Bach, Alex Smekta and Dewey Day, who was her son-in-law.

THE WEATHERBALL, 1949

Between the 1950s and the '70s, access to weather information was slower than it is today. Most people got their weather forecast with the evening news on television. Updates were rare except for severe weather alarms. Continuous reporting by the Weather Channel began in 1980. In 1949, Northwestern National Bank, which later became Norwest, then Wells Fargo, installed its first Weatherball on a tower above its main branch in Minneapolis. It was visible from fifteen miles away.

A similar device was mounted atop the sign of the Rochester branch on 2nd Street between Broadway and 1st Avenue SW. It was a translucent globe, three to four feet in diameter, lit from within. Depending on the weather forecast, the Weatherball was lit with red, white or green light. The bank advertised with its easily remembered ditties explaining the Weatherball's prediction of approaching weather:

> *When the Weatherball is glowing red / Warmer weather's just ahead.*
> *When the Weatherball is wearing green / No weather changes are foreseen.*
> *When the Weatherball is shining white / Colder weather is in sight.*
> *Sometimes it blinked: Colors blinking by night and day say /*
> *Precipitation's on the way.*

Those earworms are easy to recall forty years later. The Minneapolis Weatherball was decommissioned in 1982 after a fire destroyed the bank

The Weatherball atop Northwestern Bank at 21 2nd Street SW. *Courtesy of the* Rochester Post Bulletin.

building, though not the Weatherball. Rochester's Weatherball was decommissioned about the same time when the bank moved around the corner to the intersection of 1st Avenue and 1st Street SW.

ROCHESTER CIVIC THEATRE, 1951

The Rochester Civic Theatre (RCT) held its first organizational meetings on July 23, 1951, in the Rochester Art Center. Its first performance was Moss

Hart's *Light Up the Sky* on September 13, 1951. It was staged in the Isaac Walton log cabin on 7th Avenue NE, and the organization was then known as "The Log Cabin players." Its third play, *Two Blind Mice*, was performed at the since demolished St. Mary's Auditorium. It was incorporated in 1952 as Rochester Civic Theater. After 1952, RCT was located at 6 7th Street NW in a building that was previously a bottling plant, a truck garage and an appliance warehouse. It seated 175 but was compromised in its stage, backstage and other spaces. Seats were recycled from the old Empress Theater on South Broadway. The first staging of a musical was *Brigadoon* on September 5, 1952. Its first Children's Theater production was in 1961. Its first full-time professional director was Thom Feuerstein in 1959–60. He was followed by Jim Cavanaugh beginning in August 1960.

In 1962, supporters raised $250,000 for a Civic Theater Building Fund toward construction of the current RCT building, seating an audience of 299. It was located on space previously used for a city maintenance garage. It was initially freestanding on Center Street facing the Rochester Art Center to the east and the Mayo Civic Auditorium (as it was then known) to the south. It opened on December 6, 1963, with a performance of *South Pacific*. Like the Art Center, the completed building was given to the city and leased back for a nominal $1 per year. A later expansion of the Civic Center in the late 1990s connected to RCT with an expanded lobby and a new

Mayo Civic Center Complex circa 1960s–70s: Mayo Civic Auditorium (*center*), with Presentation Hall (*at front*), Hockey Arena (*behind*) and meeting rooms on flanks, Rochester Civic Theater (*left foreground*) and Rochester Art Center (*left background*). *Courtesy of the Rochester Post Bulletin.*

entrance. A further expansion of RCT in 2016 added a 3,300-square-foot, $4.5 million black-box theater, with seating for up to 200, on the west side of the facility. It was constructed concurrently with the Convention Center of the Mayo Civic Center. It was intended to allow different options for staging theater as well as education programs, concerts, films, art exhibits and other performances. It opened on October 21, 2016, with a production of Margaret Edson's *Wit*.

RCT was rocked in 2017 by the sudden departure of its executive director, Gregory Stavrou, and the termination of longtime artistic director Greg Miller. Complaints of sexual harassment and financial mismanagement were alleged but not publicly disclosed. Miller and RCT reached a legal settlement in 2018 but without public details. Concern was further compounded by the sudden departure of subsequent executive director Kevin Miller (no relation) in January 2020. The board was criticized, particularly by a group of former RCT supporters and volunteers, for human resource decisions that were not publicly explained to the satisfaction of some. Finances remained perilous. Meanwhile, the RCT board and staff continued efforts to rebuild support from the city council and the community and to stabilize finances while continuing to stage artistically sound productions. In the past few years, under the direction of Misha Johnson, the Civic Theater has regained credibility in the community and has developed much stronger relationships with other arts organizations.

MICHAELS, HUBBELL HOUSE AND THE PAPPAS FAMILY, 1951

During its sixty-three years of business, Michaels Restaurant was considered one of the finest restaurants in Rochester. It maintained its premier reputation in its downtown location when it was "common knowledge" that no restaurant could succeed downtown. Michaels was founded in 1951 by Michael and Mary Pappas and their four sons (George, Jim, Paul and Chuck). Known primarily for steaks and seafood, they maintained a Greek menu within their main menu, a tribute to the family's Greek heritage. In later years, although it was owned by the family collectively, it was run primarily by Chuck and later by Jim's son Michael, who founded the adjoining bar, Pappageorge's Taverna. Chuck remained engaged in the restaurant, holding off on retirement until 2014, at the age of eighty-nine, when the restaurant closed.

Michaels Restaurant & Lounge. *Courtesy of Dean Riggott Photography.*

Paul Pappas and his wife, Irene, also founded the Hubbell House in Mantorville in 1946. The three-story Mantorville landmark was a stagecoach stop and inn built of local limestone back in 1855 (168 years ago). The building was abandoned until Irene's father, Walt Stussy, acquired it by paying the back taxes.

Michaels was a favorite spot for locals as well as visitors. The office and the walls of the entry lobby were covered with celebrity photos. Returning local guests, like celebrities, could expect to be greeted by name by the maître d', usually a family member. The Hubbell House treated its guests similarly, both locals and celebrities.

Both restaurants had staff who worked there for decades and were treated like family, including several employees with significant disabilities who were accommodated with dignity. Chuck and Paul Pappas were inducted into the Minnesota Hospitality Hall of Fame in 1994.

In November 2014, the Pappas family announced that they had reached a deal with Gus Chafoulias's Titan Development to close and make way for a new development. Michaels closed after sixty-three years on New Year's Eve 2014. Nearly nine years later, the building has finally been demolished and now awaits new construction. Since 2013, Chris and Sheila Pappas have owned and managed Pappy's Place, offering "laid-back American fare" on the frontage road west of U.S. Highway 52 in northwest Rochester.

James Pappas died in 1993 at the age of seventy-six. Paul died in 1996, five days short of the Hubbell House's fiftieth anniversary. Paul's son Don and his wife, Rose, with their daughters Alaina and Kate, managed the Hubbell House for another twenty-five years until 2021, when they sold it to Rochester restaurateur and caterer Joe Powers. Chuck died in 2018 at the age of ninety-two.[113]

CRENLO, 1951

Crenlo builds cabs, hoods and other large sheet metal components for vehicles in agriculture, construction, forestry, military, mining, rail and specialty truck markets. It also had a recently sold division, Emcor Enclosures, which produces metal computer server cabinets, enclosures and consoles, mostly for the computer industry and government/defense contractors.

It was started in 1951. Three men—Roger Cresswell, John C. Enblom and William W. Lowther—used the first two letters of their last names to coin the name "Crenlo" for their new business. They started at 1600 4th Avenue NW in a 40,000-square-foot building vacated by a bankrupt Kepp Electric and Manufacturing Co. By the end of their first year, they had thirty employees and sold over $250,000 in product. Their first contract was for five hundred tractor cabs for Caterpillar. Later customers included Allis Chalmers, J.I. Case and John Deere, then IBM, 3M, Western Electric and Control Data. Crenlo has grown to the point that it currently employs over four hundred people in Rochester and has two Rochester facilities: a 420,000-square-foot building at 2501 Valleyhigh Drive NW and a 191,000-square-foot building at 1600 4th Avenue NW. It has a similar wholly owned subsidiary in South America, Siac do Brasil. UAW Local 2125 represents Crenlo's Rochester employees.

Crenlo was purchased by GF Business Equipment of Youngstown, Ohio, in 1967, but Enblom retained a large portion of preferred stock in the parent company. It continued to operate as Crenlo. In 1975, Crenlo purchased Emcor Enclosures, originally named Elgin Metal Formers Corp. It has been a division of Crenlo that produces metal server cabinets, enclosures and consoles, mostly for the computer industry and defense contractors. In October 2021, Crenlo CEO John Lenga announced the sale of Emcor Enclosures to California-based Jonathan Engineered Solutions, which makes precision ball-bearing slides, brackets, trays and sheet metal assemblies

Crenlo Inc. *Courtesy of the* Rochester Post Bulletin.

complementary to Emcor's enclosures. Emcor, with its fifty employees, was expected to continue operations at the Rochester Technology Campus, formerly the IBM campus.

Crenlo was sold in 1999 to Dover Diversified Inc. In 2011, it was purchased by New York–based KPS Capital Partners. It was sold in 2019 to Angeles Equity Partners. In the 2019 transaction, Angeles Equity Partners also acquired Worthington Industries Engineered Cabs, with facilities in Greeneville, Tennessee, and Watertown, South Dakota. Combined and operating as Crenlo Engineered Cabs, they have a total employment of 653 with annual revenues of $177.3 million.

In 2021, Angeles Equity Partners threatened to move Crenlo out of Rochester unless it received financial support from the city and state. In response, the city, through Rochester Economic Development Inc., provided a $300,000 forgivable loan. The Minnesota Investment Fund added a $450,000 forgivable loan from the state. Rochester Public Utilities offered $500,000 in rate incentives, bringing a total of $1.25 million given to Crenlo. In return, Crenlo pledged to retain 336 jobs in Rochester for five years. Crenlo has used some of the funds for a new paint line at its plant at 2501 Valleyhigh Drive NW. Crenlo announced plans to close the plant at 1600 4th Avenue NW by the end of 2021. On December 7, 2022, STORE Capital, an Arizona-based real estate trust, purchased the 4th Avenue plant plus nine acres of land for $12.65 million. The same group had purchased Crenlo's Valleyhigh Drive facility in 2021 for $21.5 million. However, in June 2023, the plant was still active.[114]

WONG'S CAFÉ, 1952

Wong's Café was founded in Rochester in 1952 by brothers Neil and Ben Wong and their spouses Poya and Mae Wong. The brothers had learned their trade working at the Canton Café, their father's restaurant in Austin, Minnesota. They bought out Bruno's Cafe at 20 Third Street SW from owner Bruno Lisi. They served traditional Cantonese cuisine as well as American menu items. In 1983, Wong's moved to a former bank building at the corner of South Broadway and 3rd Street SW. The original building now houses Mezza9 Café and Desserts after several years as the Nordic Gypsy. In 2005, Wong's moved to a new location in the Hillcrest Shopping Center and continued to operate as Wong's Café. Tessa Leung took over the site on Broadway with Sontes, a tapas restaurant. In 2021, Wong's head chef for the prior twenty-four years bought the business and changed the name to Cantonese Wong's Café with the same menu.[115]

Twin Cities Grammy-nominated jazz/rock/funk guitarist Cory Wong is Neil Wong's grandson. His most recent solo album is called *Wong's Café*. The cover illustration is a reproduction of a 1960s vintage postcard of the entrance to the original Wong's Café. In 2021, Fender released its Cory Wong Stratocaster, a signature solid body electric guitar patterned after Wong's two favorite guitars, both Stratocasters.

Wong's Café. *Courtesy of Dean Riggott Photography.*

OLMSTED MEDICAL CENTER, 1953

Olmsted Medical Center (OMC) is often said to "sit in the shadow of Mayo Clinic." However, former Olmsted Medical Group president G. Richard Geier Jr., MD, stated, "We are located southeast of the Mayo Clinic, so we are never in its shadow. However, early on a winter morning when the sun hangs low on the southeast horizon…" It may seem incongruous, in a small city with the world's greatest medical center, to have a coexisting small community–based medical center providing primary and specialty care administered by practitioners unaffiliated with the big center. Yet that community-based alternative has existed, successfully, in Rochester for over sixty-five years.

The campaign to build a community hospital was initiated by Dr. William Braasch, a retired Mayo Clinic urologist, after 1946, supporting the general practice of medicine and surgery by community physicians as an option for citizens of Olmsted County. The concept was approved by Olmsted County commissioners in 1947, and in November 1948, Olmsted County voters strongly supported a bond referendum for $750,000 to build a seventy-five-bed hospital. Planning and construction were slow. The initial proposed site was next to Bear Creek in Mayo Park. A well-timed spring flood convinced the planners to look elsewhere. Eventually, a site was chosen on eight and a

Olmsted Community Hospital. *Courtesy of the* Rochester Post Bulletin.

half acres adjacent to Rochester State Hospital (coincidentally next door to the Mayo family farm). E.W. Buenger of Ellerbe and Co. was the principal architect. Rising costs in the meantime necessitated reduction in the planned number of beds from seventy-five to fifty-five. Construction began on April 13, 1954, and finished with a dedication on June 26, 1955. The last payment on the bonds for construction was made on December 15, 1964. An addition with obstetrical wing was added in 1968, increasing the bed count to seventy-two. Cedric Linville served as the hospital administrator from the opening until he retired in 1974. When faced with the need to modernize the hospital in 1977, Olmsted County voters approved a $1.3 million referendum with over 75 percent in favor, including strong support in the city, not just among rural voters. Further expansion and renovation were approved in 1986. It is currently licensed for sixty-one beds.

In 1949, Dr. Harold "Hal" Wente opened a solo general practice office in the Lawler Cleaners building at Center Street and Broadway, just three blocks from Mayo Clinic's 1914 Building. He received a cordial reception from the community, including from Mayo Clinic, and his practice prospered and grew. In 1953, Wente joined with a group of other doctors to form Olmsted Medical Group (OMG) with a new clinic on SE 3rd Avenue. They admitted patients to and provided nonexclusive staffing to Olmsted Community Hospital.

In 1966, the Rochester Epidemiology Project was started, combining all medical records (Mayo Clinic plus OMG plus other practices) in Olmsted County, funded by National Institutes of Health, making the residents of Olmsted County the best-studied county population ever.

OMG gradually expanded, both on the southeast Rochester site and at satellite locations, the first in the new Miracle Mile. They computerized their business systems and processes early, along with several practice innovations. In 1986, OMC became the first tobacco-free medical center in Minnesota. Dr. Wente retired in 1987, but his vision persisted in the group. (He died at the age of ninety-two in 2015.) In 1996, OMG and the community hospital merged into Olmsted Medical Center, a 501(c)3 not-for-profit organization.

Since then, OMC has expanded its footprint in Rochester and across southeast Minnesota. It has over twenty-two locations, including two multi-specialty clinics (with thirty-five specialties), a walk-in clinic at Miracle Mile, the community hospital (a Level IV trauma center with twenty-four-hour ER), a Skyway Clinic and eleven community branch clinics from Wanamingo to Lake City and Cannon Falls to Preston. Recent additions include a Northwest Clinic (2010), a Sports Medicine and Athletic Performance facility (2014) and a Women's Health Pavilion (2014). It serves more than 80,000 unique patients each year. It employs over 1,372 healthcare professionals, including 189 clinicians. As a not-for-profit organization, it returns its net revenue to the community. (In 2020, OMC made community contributions of over $68 million, 31 percent of its total operating expenses.)[116]

Fig Leaf, 1954

Mayo Clinic's art collection is extensive. One of its most iconic artworks is Ivan Mestrovic's twenty-eight-foot-tall cast-bronze statue *Man and Freedom*, which was mounted on the north wall of the Mayo Building until 2001. When the Gonda Building was attached to the north face, the statue was taken down from the original mount, refinished for indoor exhibit and rehung lower and to the east on the same wall, now overlooking the Landau Atrium of the Gonda.

Man and Freedom, like Michelangelo's *David*, is depicted nude, but unlike the *David* as currently exhibited, has a fig leaf covering his genitalia, as was commonly practiced in Europe for centuries since the Council of Trent in 1563 banned "all lasciviousness" in religious images. The seventy-year-old maquette (small demonstration model of a proposed sculpture) for *Man and Freedom* still exists in the collection of Mayo Clinic in Phoenix, Arizona. It does not have a fig leaf, which raises a question about the originality of the fig leaf. The participants in the production and the acquisition of the statue are no longer alive, but in a recent communication with G. Slade Schuster Jr., the son of G. Slade Schuster Sr. (head of Section of Administration of Mayo Clinic from 1953 to 1970), he wrote: "My father went out to inspect the statue when it arrived by truck. Mestrovic, the sculptor, had not put a fig leaf on the original. Father took one look and said, 'This is Minnesota; we can't have an icicle hanging from THAT all winter.' He sent it back and it now has a fig leaf. It sounds like dad anyway."[117]

Roy Watson Sr. and Jr., 1955

For fifty-four years, the hospitality industry in Rochester was led by Roy Watson Sr. and Jr. This was confusing because IBM was led by two Watsons during the same era. Thomas John Watson Sr. (February 17, 1874–June 19, 1956) and Thomas John Watson Jr. (January 14, 1914–December 31, 1993) were the first (1914–56) and second (1952–71) president/CEO of IBM.

Roy Watson Sr. grew up in western Wisconsin, the son of a hotel and tavern operator. He grew up in the business, working as a dishwasher and bellhop. He moved to Rochester in 1910. He quickly became the protege of John Kahler and worked his way up through the ranks. In 1926, he became general manager of the Kahler Hotel. When Kahler died in January 1931, Watson Sr. took over as president/CEO of Kahler Corporation from which he retired in 1955. He retired from the board in 1960. He died on September 7, 1966.

Roy Sr. and his family were the first inhabitants (from December 16, 1933, to November 2, 1944) of the house that I grew up in at 853 8th Avenue SW.

Roy Jr. was born in the Damon Hotel on October 22, 1921, graduated from Rochester High School in 1939 and became an Eagle Scout in 1940. He received degrees from Dartmouth College (economics and political science) in 1943 and Cornell University (hotel management) in 1948. He

Roy Watson Sr. and Jr. *Courtesy of the History Center of Olmsted County.*

served as lieutenant commander of USS *Makassar Strait*, which fought in both the battles of Iwo Jima and Okinawa.

He served as general manager of the Kahler Hotel and president and board chair of the Kahler Corp. from 1955 to 1982 (starting at age thirty-three!). He served as president of the Minnesota Motel & Hotel Association, 1955; president of the American Hotel & Motel Association, 1964; president of Honor Inter-American Hotel Association, 1973; and vice president of the International Hotel Association, 1976.

He was actively involved in the community with leadership roles in the American Legion, Rochester Chamber & Junior Chamber of Commerce, Rochester Youth Football, Baseball and Hockey Associations (director and coach). He served on the boards of the Olmsted County History Center and Rochester Methodist Hospital (1954–1980). He chaired the committee that advocated for the Mayo Centennial stamp in 1964 and served as president of both the Rochester Park Board (1969–81, during which parks facilities dramatically expanded, including the civic center, golf courses, rec center and other facilities and parks) and the Olmsted County Park Board (2005–11). The soccer complex in northwest Rochester is named in his honor.

Roy Jr. was a great local personality, renowned for his storytelling. He could "schmooze" with VIP guests of the Kahler and had a huge collection of portrait photos of celebrities, including John F. Kennedy, Lyndon Johnson, Charles Lindbergh, Saudi King Faisal, Admiral Richard E. Byrd, Helen Keller, Jesse Owens, Jack Dempsey, Lou Gehrig, Joe DiMaggio, Jack Benny, Groucho Marx, Frank Sinatra, Lee Marvin and hundreds more. His distinctive house on Memorial Parkway SW is a Cape Cod cottage designed by Francis Underwood and built in 1957. He died on September 10, 2012, and is buried in Oakwood Cemetery.[118]

THE FIEGEL FAMILY AND TOM WATSON'S DECISION TO BUILD THE IBM PLANT IN ROCHESTER, 1956

In 1956, when presented a choice to build a new IBM plant in either Rochester, Minnesota, or Madison, Wisconsin, CEO Tom Watson Jr. chose Rochester as a tribute to Leland Fiegel, a Rochester native who was a decorated World War II bomber pilot who flew a critical mission to Moscow with Watson at the start of the war.[119]

Lester John Fiegel Sr. was born on September 14, 1884, in Salem Township, to John Albert and Ella Mary Fiegel. He grew up on the family farm and received his business education at Darling's Business College in Rochester. From 1908 to 1911, he served as elected Salem township assessor while also teaching in rural schools. In 1912, he was elected Olmsted County auditor, a role in which he served for eight years. He married Anna Eleanor Kenitz on December 28, 1912, in Wabasha. They had two sons and four daughters and twenty-one grandchildren. In 1920, he joined First National Bank as a cashier. He rose through the ranks and was elected to the role of vice president in 1932, in which he served until retirement in 1950. He then worked in real estate and the insurance business for three years before joining Olmsted County Bank & Trust as president, where he served seven more years, then retired again in 1960 at age seventy-five. He was an active member of the community, serving as secretary of the Selective Service Board during World War I, treasurer of Olmsted County Historical Society (1926–52), member of the Rochester School Board (1926–32), a charter member and in 1922 president of Kiwanis, president of the advisory unit on construction of new courthouse, the Rochester Charter Commission for five years, Rochester Methodist Hospital Board, the board of directors of Mayo Memorial Association and numerous other organizations. In March 1928, he was a founding investor in Rochester Airways, which built one of Rochester's early airports at 2305 2nd Street SW. That small field was quickly replaced the same year by what was later known as Lobb Field in southeast Rochester. Lobb Field was sponsored by Rochester Airport Company, a subsidiary of Mayo Properties Association, with far more capital and a seven times larger field. Several years later, Fiegel bought the 2nd Street property, 80 acres (one-quarter by one-half mile), which his family called "the ranch." It subsequently became the Rochester Golf Range and later was sold to a sand mining interest and eventually became the Shorewood Senior Campus and the southern part of Cascade Lake Park. Lester Sr. died on November 17, 1969, in Rochester at the age of eighty-five and is buried in Oakwood Cemetery. A memorial on the east shore of Cascade Lake Park was dedicated in his honor on August 14, 2021.[120]

Leland Gordon Fiegel (March 13, 1914–April 28, 1948) was the eldest of six children of Lester and Anna Fiegel. He was inspired to become a pilot, perhaps as early as 1928, but certainly by 1933 when he attended the Chicago World's Fair. He graduated from the University of Minnesota in 1936, joined the U.S. Army Air Corps (which became the Air Force after World War II) and was appointed second lieutenant and received his

Left: Colonel Leland Gordon Fiegel (1914–1948). *Courtesy of the family of Colonel Leland Fiegel.*

Below: B-24 Liberator heavy bomber on new tarmac at Rochester Airport, April 15, 1942. *Courtesy of the family of Colonel Leland Fiegel.*

pilot's wings in June 1937. In November 1940, Fiegel was appointed aide to Brigadier General Follett Bradley. On February 25, 1942, Bradley was promoted to major general (three stars) and in March was appointed as commanding general of the First Air Force. Bradley later described Fiegel as "one of the best pilots I have ever known."[121]

On April 15, 1942, Captain Fiegel and his crew took off from Barksdale Field near Shreveport, Louisiana, at 11:20 a.m. in their four-engine Consolidated B-24 Liberator heavy bomber. They landed at the Rochester airport at 3:00 p.m. Fiegel and Anna Mae Towey were married at St. John's Parish house at 5:30 p.m. A reception followed at the Kahler Hotel. That evening, over one thousand Rochester residents cheered as Fiegel and his crew took off from Rochester Airport at 8:10 p.m. for a four-hour and thirty-seven-minute return flight to back to Shreveport. The bride followed the next day by commercial aircraft.[122]

In 1942, at the age of twenty-eight, Major Fiegel was chosen by Major General Bradley to fly a B-24 Liberator on a critical mission to Moscow. Bradley's adjutant, and Fiegel's copilot for the mission, was Lieutenant Colonel Tom Watson Jr., the son of the first chairman and CEO of IBM.[123] They became close friends. They took a complex around-the-world route to Moscow on the lengthy mission to support negotiations by Bradley and Wendell Willkie with Stalin and Churchill to "arrange for the delivery via

Crew of the MOCKBA in Moscow: Major Thomas Watson Jr. (*far left*) Major General Follett Bradley (*third from left*) and Major Leland Fiegel (*far right*). *Courtesy of the family of Colonel Leland Fiegel.*

140

Alaska of War-Aid airplanes to Siberia and Russia" and exchange of related information as part of the Lend-Lease Program.[124] While there, the team was entertained well, including a performance at the Moscow Conservatory of Dmitri Shostakovich's new Seventh (Leningrad) Symphony.[125] After successfully concluding negotiations, and to celebrate this bond with our allies, the Soviets, General Bradley had the nose of the bomber lettered MOCKBA ("Moscow" in Russian). On the return trip to the USA, the crew stopped in China for negotiations with Chiang Kai-shek, then flew on via Siberia and the Aleutians back to Canada and the United States. They nearly crashed their B-24 when it iced up flying out of Yakutsk, Siberia. They were forced to return and abandon the disabled B-24 to the Siberian winter and fly home with a loaned cargo plane. On return to the United States, on December 2, 1942, they landed in Rochester, where the Fiegel family hosted the entire Bradley party for dinner at the University Club at the Kahler Hotel.[126]

Major Fiegel was awarded the Distinguished Flying Cross for the Moscow mission in March 1943. His citation was awarded in Pyote, Texas, by General Davenport Johnson, commander of the Second Air Force. It read:

> *For meritorious achievement while participating in an aerial flight from Washington, D.C., to Yakutsk, Siberia, via South America, Africa, Middle East, Russia and China, during the period of July 26, 1942, to November 21, 1942, on a highly important military mission to Russia. With no thought of personal hardship consequent to flying on this flight and repeated flights made within the Soviet Union under conditions made hazardous by extremely adverse weather conditions, the proximity of enemy aircraft over parts of the routes, inaccurate maps, inadequate communications and maintenance facilities, and dangerous overload conditions, he displayed conspicuous skill, courage, initiative, and good judgment in the performance of his duties, thereby contributing greatly to the success of the mission.*

During the war, Fiegel served in the Eighth Air Force in England, commanded by General James Doolittle. Fiegel commanded the Ninety-Third Bomb Group, half of the twentieth wing (one of five wings) of the Second Division (with fifty thousand men) of the Eighth Air Force. The Ninety-Third flew bombing missions in B-24 Liberator heavy bombers. The Ninety-Third was nicknamed "Ted's Flying Circus" after its first commander, Brigadier General Edward J. "Ted" Timberlake Jr. The group had a poor performance record before Fiegel took charge but improved substantially under Fiegel's command. On September 27, 1943, Fiegel was promoted to a full colonel. In February 1944, the group received the Distinguished Unit Citation after completing 100 missions over enemy territory in Europe, Egypt and the Middle East. Fiegel received a second oak leaf cluster for his DFC award in 1944. By the end of the war, the Ninety-Third Bomb Group was the oldest B-24 Liberator group in Europe and had flown the most bombing missions of any B-24 group with the lowest rate of casualties. While flying 396 missions and 8,169 sorties, they lost only 100 airplanes. Fiegel received the Air Medal with three oak leaf clusters. In October 1944, Fiegel was made chief of staff of the Eighth Air Force combat wing under Brigadier General Timberlake. In May 1945, he received a commendation from Brigadier General Timberlake for his leadership, under which the "overall efficiency of the 93rd Bombardment Group increased from a state of mediocrity to that of superior standards."[127]

After the war, Fiegel and Watson remained friends. Watson joined IBM and succeeded his father as president in 1952 and CEO in 1956. Fiegel stayed in the air force as a colonel and assistant director of air force training in the Pentagon. He participated in the separation of the air force as a military branch distinct from the army. In 1948, while fulfilling his monthly quota of flying hours, he flew a twin-engine Beechcraft C-45 to Mitchell Field in New York to visit Tom Watson at IBM headquarters. On April 28, 1948, on the return flight to Bolling Field near Washington, D.C., the Beechcraft lost an engine and exploded in midair near Prince Frederick, Maryland, killing Fiegel and two crew members. He was buried on April 30 in Arlington National Cemetery and was posthumously awarded the British Distinguished Flying Cross for heroic service during World War II. He left behind his wife, Anna Mae, and two sons: John (age five) and Richard (age one). Watson maintained communications with the Fiegels, and in May 1964, the Watsons hosted both Lester Sr. and Lester Jr. at their home in Greenwich, Connecticut.[128] Watson visited the Fiegels in Rochester in March 1965 and again in 1968. They maintained a friendly correspondence throughout these years.

In 1956, IBM considered options for a new plant site. The initial proposal did not include Rochester as an option. Tom Watson Jr. had succeeded his father as CEO by then. He recommended that Rochester be considered. A consultant then reviewed the large number of options and narrowed the choice to Madison, Wisconsin, versus Rochester, Minnesota. "When presented the two options, Watson asked the consultant if the two choices were relatively equal. When the answer was yes, he said, 'Well then, we'll go to Rochester, Minnesota.' He telephoned Leland Fiegel's father, Lester J. Fiegel Sr., in Rochester to tell him the choice made in honor of his son and Watson's close friend. This news was kept private by the Fiegels until IBM was ready to publicize it." Rochester business leaders had recently formed Industrial Opportunities Inc., of which Fiegel Sr. was a charter member. It was created to solicit new businesses for Rochester. They received news of the new IBM plant as a *fait accompli*. IBM had already purchased two farms for its campus just north of the edge of town. "Watson came to Rochester to make the announcement himself. He also visited the Fiegel family, including Lester J. Fiegel, Jr. Watson later disclosed the Fiegel connection when he returned to Rochester to address the Mayo Medical School graduation in 1987. The *Post Bulletin* Answer Man column addressed the attribution in September 2022 and concluded that that the Fiegel connection was unproven. He was promptly contacted by Audrey Fiegel Higgins Garbish, Leland Fiegel's sole surviving sibling, and provided with additional evidence including a scrapbook full of *Post Bulletin* articles, correspondence with Watson, and a tape recording from Tom Watson documenting Watson's "tribute to his friendship with Leland and the Fiegel family." One of the articles quoted Watson saying of Fiegel, "I admired him as much as any man I ever knew."[129]

IBM campus in Rochester, Minnesota. *Courtesy of Dean Riggott Photography.*

Colonel Leland Fiegel memorial in Oakwood Cemetery. *Courtesy of the family of Colonel Leland Fiegel.*

Leland Fiegel's brother Lester J. Fiegel Jr. (Lec to family, Les to coworkers) was seventeen years his junior, born in 1931. He grew up in Rochester and married Jacqueline Aird in 1953. Together, they had three children: Scott (my high school classmate and friend), Kirby and Anne. He received his bachelor's degree in electrical engineering from the University of Minnesota in 1956 and moved to Poughkeepsie, New York, to work for IBM. He was transferred to the plant in Rochester, his hometown, where he raised his family and stayed until moving to Austin, Texas, in 1980 to finish his thirty-five-year career with IBM. He died in 2011. His ashes are in the Fiegel family plot in Oakwood Cemetery beside his grandparents, parents and three older siblings.[130] Among the gravestones is a similar stone marker as a memorial for Leland.

A.M. "SANDY" KEITH, 1959

Alexander MacDonald "Sandy" Keith is believed to be the first person in Minnesota to serve in key roles of all three branches of state government. He served as state senator (1959–63), lieutenant governor (1963–67) and justice of the Minnesota Supreme Court (associate, 1989–90; chief, 1990–98).

Keith was a Rochester native, born on November 22, 1928, to Dr. Norman M. and Edna Keith. His father was a Canadian-born Mayo Clinic physician. In 1950, Keith graduated magna cum laude from Amherst College, where

Minnesota Supreme Court chief justice A.M. "Sandy" Keith. *Courtesy of the History Center of Olmsted County.*

he was a star football player and New England wrestling champion as well as a member of Phi Beta Kappa. He graduated from Yale Law School in 1953, then served in the U.S. Marine Corps, including a year in Korea as a first lieutenant during the Korean War. He married Marion E. Sanford on April 29, 1955. They had two sons, Ian and Douglas, and four grandchildren. From 1955 to 1960, he served on the legal staff of Mayo Clinic as associate counsel, working with future U.S. Supreme Court justice Harry Blackmun.

In 1959, Keith was elected as a member of the Democratic-Farmer-Labor Party (DFL) to the Minnesota Senate. The following year, he served as a delegate to the Democratic National Convention. In 1962, he ran for lieutenant governor with Karl Rolvaag. They served together from 1963 until 1967. In 1966, he challenged Rolvaag for the DFL nomination for governor but was defeated by Rolvaag in the primary election.

From 1967 to 1989, he ran a busy practice of family law in Rochester with a strong emphasis on mediation.

In 1989, Keith was appointed associate justice of the Minnesota Supreme Court by Governor Rudy Perpich. A year later, Chief Justice Peter S. Popovich retired, and Keith was appointed to succeed him as chief justice, a role he continued until retiring in 1998 at the mandatory age of seventy.

In retirement, Keith remained active in the community. He was the first president of Greater Rochester Area University Center (GRAUC), a group that advocated successfully for establishment of a branch of the University of Minnesota in Rochester. He helped form the Rochester Downtown Alliance (RDA) and became its first executive director from 2005 to 2010. The Sandy Keith Award was established by the RDA in 2017 to honor individuals who have made a notable impact on downtown Rochester. Keith was the inaugural recipient.

Keith was always friendly and approachable. His good friend John Wade described how Keith "would often stop by Wade's home around dinner time and walk in without knocking. He'd sit down, grab some food and start recounting whatever story was on his mind."[131]

He died on October 3, 2020, at his home in Rochester. He was ninety-four.

Ernest Hemingway, 1960

"Rochester holds the distinction of being the last new place Hemingway would ever travel to."[132] He was treated here for depression shortly before he died by suicide.

Ernest Hemingway (July 21, 1899–July 2, 1961) is considered one of the greatest American writers. He published novels, short stories and works of journalism, particularly war correspondence, mainly from the mid-1920s to the early 1950s. He was renowned for his concise, unadorned writing style. In describing his writing style, he said to one of his Mayo Clinic physicians: "Hugh, you go home tonight with this book [*The Old Man and the Sea*] and open it. Close your eyes and put your finger down on any page you come to. Then you sit down and try to shorten the sentence." He was awarded the Nobel Prize for Literature in 1954. His lifestyle was legendary: married four times with many love affairs, war correspondent, big game hunter, deep sea fisherman, world traveler, excessive drinker, boxer, friend of the stars, larger-than-life personality.

In 1960, at the age of sixty-one, he was living in Ketchum, Idaho, with his fourth wife, Mary Welsh. His lifestyle had apparently taken its toll. In addition to the physical residua from two nearly fatal plane crashes in 1954, he suffered from depression and paranoid delusions. He lost weight and strength, found himself unable to write and felt he was losing his memory. He became suicidal. His local physician recommended an evaluation at the Menninger Clinic in Topeka, Kansas, but he declined. He eventually agreed to a referral to Mayo Clinic. He was admitted to St. Mary's Hospital, and Mary checked into the Kahler, both under aliases.

He was treated from November 30, 1960, to January 22, 1961. The first thing his physicians did was discontinue his antihypertensive, reserpine, which causes depression. But that did not improve his depression. Several antidepressant medications were tried, and he was treated with electroconvulsive therapy (ECT or electroshock therapy). He was remarkably free to roam around the city during his treatments and became familiar with the homes and families of several of his physicians. He was frequently seen walking around the city and out to the outskirts of town. It was rumored that he frequented downtown bars, particularly the Pinnacle Room at the Kahler.

In early January he was thought to be improved, so ECT was discontinued. He was discharged home on January 22. On return to Ketchum, he seemed improved but was still unable to write. He gradually deteriorated. He was already anxious about his financial security. The CIA invasion of Cuba at the Bay of Pigs on April 15 assured the loss of his home outside Havana, which contained many of his most prized possessions, his personal reference library and three major unfinished manuscripts. He became actively suicidal again. He was taken back to Mayo Clinic and readmitted on April 25 to St. Mary's in the locked psychiatric ward. He was given more ECT treatments. He complained that his memory was worse, although that is a common temporary effect of ECT. After a while, he assured his physicians that he would not harm himself, and they liberalized his restrictions. He resumed his walking about and visiting the homes of his physicians. He became a common sight around southwest Rochester. In one instance, he asked a host if he could do something useful outside, so they allowed him to mow their lawn. Upon seeing him mowing the lawn, a neighbor commented: "The Rynearsons' have a gardener who looks exactly like Ernest Hemingway."

In late June, he convinced his psychiatrist that he was improved. Despite Mary's strong reservations, he was discharged on June 26 and drove back to Ketchum over five days. He still had paranoid delusions. Three days after returning home, in the early morning hours of July 2, he took out his favorite shotgun and killed himself.

Over sixty years later, his Mayo Clinic medical records remain confidential, but there has been continued speculation about alternative diagnoses such as bipolar disorder, chronic traumatic encephalopathy (CTE, he had had nearly a dozen concussions, one as recently as the year before), hemochromatosis and early stage dementia. Likewise, many have disputed the wisdom of his treatments. A contributing role for alcoholism is widely accepted. Otherwise, there is little consensus beyond the tragedy of his death.[133]

CELEBRITY ANECDOTE, 1961

The lobbies of Mayo Clinic often provide interesting contrasts between the wealthy or famous and people of humble origins as they wait side by side for medical appointments. In the early days of the clinic, the arrivals of celebrities were reported in the local paper. Both Michaels Restaurant and the Kahler Hotel kept celebrity portraits of their guests, most of whom were in town because of Mayo Clinic.

Stapleton Kearns is a New England landscape painter who grew up in Rochester. A 1970 graduate of Mayo High School, he was known by his first name, David, until a college professor complained of "too many Davids" in a class and asked someone to use a different name, at which point Stapleton began to use his middle name (his mother's maiden name, a southern tradition) and has since been known by that name. He shared the following reminiscence from childhood:

"My late father, Dr. Thomas P. Kearns drove an elderly hump shaped Buick, which must have been from the forties, back and forth from work. He only owned three cars that I recall, each for about twenty-five years. The Buick had a leather covered rope that hung across the back of the front seat. I guess it was supposed to help you get in and out. My dad pulled out the back seat and filled the car with leaves he had raked from our yard and took them to the dump. I remember the dump. It was a huge smoldering hole in the ground. You backed your car up and threw your trash over the edge. The next morning, he drove to work without replacing the seat or cleaning out the car. He was a very orderly and fastidious man, and I am surprised he would do that, but perhaps he planned to make another dump trip.

After working at the clinic for the morning, he was leaving through the staff entrance to go down to St. Mary's Hospital. A more senior physician asked him to drive 'a couple of guys' there as a favor. My father tried to explain that he had his back seat removed and the car was a mess, but the older doctor told him the 'guys' were in a hurry and wouldn't care. My father ran up the street to a parking lot across from the old library and drove back to the clinic. The passengers waiting for him were Whitey Ford and Mickey Mantle. They climbed in and squatted in the back hanging onto the leather covered rope for balance. At St. Mary's they cheerfully thanked my father for the lift and climbed out. Dad told me he watched them going up the steps to the hospital brushing the dried leaves from the bottoms of their long tweed coats."[134]

"The Greatest Doctor in the World," 1965

The supply of humility occasionally runs a little short within the medical profession. A prominent Mayo Clinic physician of a past generation never claimed to be humble. Dr. Edward H. Rynearson (1901–1987) was a Mayo Clinic endocrinologist, widely renowned as a clinical endocrinologist, lecturer and early advocate for humane end-of-life care. His contemporary Dr. Victor Johnson told of an instance when Rynearson was attending a national scientific meeting: "Conversation turned toward discussion of the

Dr. Edward Rynearson, "The Greatest Doctor in the World." *Used with permission of Mayo Foundation for Medical Education and Research.*

truly great of medical history. Someone ventured to question, 'And who would we consider to be the greatest doctor in the world today?' Without hesitation, Eddie said, 'I am. And I can prove it.' He had a bellboy get a plain postcard on which he wrote a simple query such as, 'I would like your help.' He addressed the card to 'The Greatest Doctor in the World,' and assured them all he would receive this card, which he asked the bellboy to post. The federal postal authorities go to great extremes to try to deliver poorly addressed mail. They pondered a while, and then it occurred to them that probably the great Mayo Clinic may know who the greatest doctor in the world might be. The Clinic's mail clerk who received the inquiry thought at once, 'This looks to me like one of Rynearson's stunts.' Eddie got the postcard."[135]

ROCHESTER EPIDEMIOLOGY PROJECT, 1966

In 1966, the Rochester Epidemiology Project (REP) was started by Dr. Leonard Kurland, a Mayo Clinic neurologist, and colleagues. It combined access to all medical records (Mayo Clinic plus Olmsted Medical Center plus other practices) in Olmsted County, making the (roughly 75,000 then, 163,000 now) residents of Olmsted County one of the best-studied populations ever from a health perspective.

The REP used resources first developed by Henry Plummer and Mabel Root in the Mayo Clinic system of medical records. It provided searchable indexes for medical diagnoses and surgical procedures. That Plummer-Root record system was enhanced in 1935 by Dr. Joseph Berkson, chief of the Division of Biometry and Medical Statistics, who introduced a unique searchable system of diagnostic codes and a punch card indicator of local residency, setting the stage for epidemiologic studies.

Kurland obtained funding from the National Institutes of Health to create a medical records linkage system with other medical facilities in Olmsted County to develop accurate data on the frequency and natural history of virtually any disease process. Since then, the study has followed all consenting

Dr. Leonard Kurland, founder of the Rochester Epidemiology Project. *Used with permission of Mayo Foundation for Medical Education and Research.*

Olmsted County residents, including over 620,000 total individuals over 50 years, with over 6 million person-years of follow-up. In recent years, the records of medical practices in 27 counties of southeast Minnesota and southwest Wisconsin have been added to expand the potential study population to 1.8 million individuals. The data can be used, for virtually any disease process, for incidence and prevalence studies, case-control studies, cohort studies, cost-effectiveness studies and outcome studies.

The REP has been continuously funded by the National Institutes of Health (NIH) since 1966 (fifty-six years). The study currently supports 408 research projects funded under a total of 39 federal grants plus other funding sources. In 2012, the REP annual budget was just under $1.4 million, 56 percent from NIH and the rest from Mayo Clinic research funding.

Olmsted County is thought to be nearly ideal for such a study, despite its lack of diversity in the past, because it is relatively isolated from other metropolitan areas and most residents receive virtually all their medical care within the county. "Olmsted County is one of the few places in the world where the occurrence and natural history of diseases can be accurately described and analyzed in a defined population for a half century or more."

Studies of the Olmsted County population have resulted in over 2,600 scientific publications regarding a great variety of medical conditions. These studies are particularly noted for establishing realistic estimates of the incidence and prevalence of various diseases in a well-defined population. The best-known REP studies evaluated heart failure, valvular heart diseases, deep vein thrombosis and pulmonary embolism, atrial fibrillation, gastroesophageal reflux, epilepsy, vertebral fractures, exophthalmic goiter and multiple sclerosis. Other studies have included cardiovascular disease, stroke, numerous cancers (e.g., breast, colon, lung, multiple myeloma), COVID-19, diabetes, asthma, pneumonia and other lung diseases, Alzheimer's disease, Parkinson's disease, rheumatoid arthritis, congenital malformations, spontaneous abortions and many other diseases and disorders.

The REP is considered unique "because of its long and complex history, its coverage of an entire population, its geographic location, and its scientific productivity."[136]

JUDY ONOFRIO, 1967

The best-known artist in Rochester is Judy Onofrio. A sculptor, she started working with ceramics in the 1970s and evolved continually in her style and materials. An avid collector of antiques, beads, buttons and many other varieties of "cool stuff," she incorporates beautiful and interesting materials and shapes into her art. A detailed biography and chronological display of her work is available on her website: www.judyonofrio.com.

She was born in New London, Connecticut, the daughter of a U.S. Navy admiral. Her family moved every two years, which she credits for her love of change. Her home environment was very strict and formal but she often escaped to visit her great-aunt Trude, an outsider artist who provided a much less structured and more exploratory environment for her. She cites her childhood experiences collecting treasures on the beach as being influential in her art. She attended Sullins College in Bristol, Virginia, where she studied business law and economics. She considers herself a self-taught artist and acknowledges influence by the works of outsider

Judy Onofrio during a visit at her home by feminist arts activists "The Guerrilla Girls." *Photo by Paul David Scanlon.*

artists (particularly Watts Tower in Los Angeles; the Dickeyville Grotto in Dickeyville, Wisconsin; and the Grotto of the Redemption in West Bend, Iowa) in her style and practice.

She moved to Rochester, Minnesota, for the first time in 1960 with her husband, Burton, a Mayo Clinic resident in neurosurgery. She was stimulated by artist Bill Saltzman and the creative environment of the Rochester Art Center. She began painting regularly when she and Burton moved back to Washington, D.C., in 1964. In 1967, they moved back to Rochester after Burton completed his military duty and joined the staff of Mayo Clinic in Neurosurgery. She acknowledges Burton's total support for "every crazy idea I've ever had." In 1970, she became more involved with her art, primarily ceramics. She became acting director of the Rochester Art Center (RAC) and the founding director of Total Arts Day Camp (TADC), a children's summer art program, now in its fifty-third year. TADC became an influential model of arts education, introducing children to professional artists and providing for the creation of real art. After B.J. Shigaki became director of RAC, Onofrio continued to support and guide the institution for many years as a member of its board of directors.

Beginning working with clay in the early 1970s, she developed a strong network of artist friends throughout Minnesota and nearby states, including Don Reitz, Warren MacKenzie, Curt Hoard, Walter Nottingham, Carole Fisher and Jim Tanner. Her work evolved. For a period, she created outdoor installations for "fire performances" with constructions of combustible materials that were set afire.

Gradually, she branched out in her artistic practice. Partly in response to outsider art installations, she began to incorporate intriguing materials and shapes from her extensive collections into jewelry, both brooches and bracelets, as well as mosaics and larger sculptures. The brooches were particularly popular among art collectors and museums. She continues to make beaded jewelry in off-hours as a form of meditative relaxation.

During the 1990s she produced a multitude of large colorful multimedia sculptures with circus-like imagery and whimsical names. One major exhibition in 2008 was titled *Ringmaster: Judy Onofrio, and the Art of the Circus* at the Chazen Museum of Art in Madison, Wisconsin. To highlight her works, she used painted panels and other circus imagery on loan from the Ringling Brothers' Circus World Museum in Baraboo, Wisconsin.

"Judyland" has been used in the titles of several exhibitions of her works, most notably a major exhibit at Minneapolis Institute of Art in 1993. But she uses the term most commonly to refer to the back garden at her home, a wonderland nature space accented by sculptures, treasures from "junk-shopping" and interesting objects from a variety of sources.

After 2000, she began to incorporate bones in many of her works, celebrating life and death. A 2010 Mayo Clinic exhibit titled *Stories of Reclining Women* addressed the experience of illness and recovery. From 2009 to 2019, she created wall-mounted medallions, baskets and other freestanding forms in very subdued colors (sometimes monochromatic). She said, "These works are largely abstract assemblages that combine animal bones, decorative architectural elements, and hand-carved fruit. Working with animal bones makes me increasingly aware of their organic beauty and the life they once supported. In this series, fertility and eroticism live side by side with mortality and fragility. It is my hope that this work will evoke the memory of the Garden of Eden and the ongoing cycle of ever-changing life. For me, this work is about my healing process and the celebration of being fully alive." Since then, prompted by the COVID-19 pandemic, she has transitioned "from Bones to Bliss" and has resumed use of a rich palate of colors and a large selection of life forms, particularly sea life, but she still incorporates bone, horn, seashells and other "remains" in her works.

Although she is self-taught and has affinity for outsider art, she is held in high regard among arts academicians. At a 2015 exhibit at St. Olaf College in celebration of Professor Ron Gallas, Onofrio participated as an exhibitor and discussion panelist. She was treated as one of two celebrities, along with Gallas. She sometimes claims, jokingly, to have a PhD from the University of Mars. She is knowledgeable, analytical and articulate in discussing contemporary art and is clearly a thought leader among academicians.

Onofrio has been well recognized in Rochester with major solo exhibits at Rochester Art Center in 1971, 2006 and 2016, the exhibit at Mayo Clinic in 2010 and other public displays of her art. Major exhibitions of her work have been hosted by Minneapolis Institute of Art; Weisman Art Museum at the University of Minnesota; Thomas Barry Fine Arts in Minneapolis; Sherry Leedy Contemporary Art in Kansas City, Missouri; North Dakota Museum of Art in Grand Forks; Plains Art Museum in Fargo, North Dakota; Arkansas Arts Center in Little Rock; and many others. The 2006 show *Come One, Come All* traveled to four cities over a year.

She has received numerous awards, including a 1978 Minnesota State Arts Board Fellowship, a McKnight Foundation Fellowship in 1995, a Bush Artists Fellowship in 1999, Lifetime Achievement Awards from Rochester Art Center in 2000 and Minnesota Crafts Council in 2001. In 2005, she received the McKnight Foundation Distinguished Artist Award.

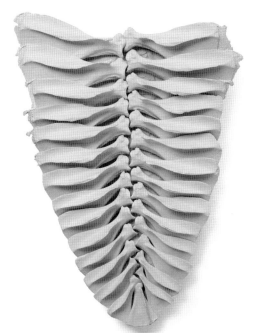

Left: *Breathe* by Judy Onofrio, 2014. *Courtesy of Judy Onofrio*.

Below: *Full Lunch*, by Judy Onofrio, 2022. *Courtesy of Judy Onofrio*.

Onofrio is highly regarded over a wide area. In 2014, she was featured on the TPT/PBS show *MN Original*. Her influence extends throughout the Midwest to Chicago, New York, Los Angeles and beyond the United States. Her works are included in many collections and museums nationally and internationally. Her principal commercial outlet is Sherry Leedy Contemporary Art in Kansas City, Missouri.[137]

Prank, 1968

Mayo High School opened its doors in the fall of 1966. The early years of a new school are often lean in athletic triumphs and trophy cases are largely empty. Mayo had a successful football campaign in the fall of 1968 with six victories to three defeats. Sadly, one of those defeats was the most important game of the season, not homecoming but the battle against crosstown rival John Marshall. JM won a closely contested game by score of 13-7. The sting of defeat was somewhat mitigated for Mayo fans by a prank. A week or two before the game, in the dead of night, a small group of students from Mayo's class of '69 climbed fences to enter what is now called John Drews Field at John Marshall. They brought bags of fertilizer and fertilizer spreaders. Surreptitiously, they spread the fertilizer in a pattern spelling "M-A-Y-O" in giant letters on the field. On the night of the big game, luxuriant green grass spelled out the name, clearly legible to outraged JM fans in the stands. The perpetrators were never identified or brought to justice.

Nudes in the Schools' Pools, 1969

A topic of recurring fascination on Facebook, in local legend and at least twice in *Post-Bulletin*'s Answer Man column (2003 and 2007) is the 1960s requirement that boys in physical education classes (but not girls, who were provided with baggy unstylish tank suits) swim nude in the pools of junior and senior public high schools in Rochester.

Answer Man confirmed, "For years, boys at Rochester high schools wore only their birthday suits in the pool for phy. ed. According to Dick Thatcher, who coached swimming at John Marshall and Mayo high schools, the dress code changed, and boys donned swimsuits in 1966, when Mayo High School

Downtown viewed from southeast, historic area in foreground. *Courtesy of Dean Riggott Photography.*

opened; the girls' locker room was too close to the pool to allow swimming in the buff. When asked why the boys swam naked prior to that, Thatcher told former P-B sportswriter Bob Brown, 'Why not?' He noted that Rochester Swim Club athletes also skinny dipped at that time."[138] As a 1971 graduate of Mayo High School, I can confirm that as a seventh through ninth grader at Central JHS in 1965–68 we swam nude in gym class. We also swam nude in tenth grade at Mayo High School in 1968–69.

SENATOR NANCY BRATAAS, 1975

Nancy Brataas served Rochester and Olmsted County as a state senator for seventeen years and as a political activist and political advisor for much longer.[139] She advised and managed political campaigns for President Richard Nixon, former Minnesota governor Arne Carlson and many others, including me. She was a member of an apparently extinct class, a pro-choice Republican. She was a fierce competitor, sometimes called "the dragon lady" by her admirers and worse by her political enemies. Extremely intelligent,

Senator Nancy Brataas.
Courtesy of the Rochester
Post Bulletin.

well-spoken and well-organized, she was always prepared for political battle.

Nancy Osborn was born in Minneapolis on January 19, 1928, and graduated from Sea Breeze High School in Daytona Beach, Florida, where she was voted "Most Likely to Succeed." She attended the University of Minnesota, majoring in art history. On November 27, 1948, she married Mark Gerard "Jerry" Brataas, a World War II Navy pilot. They moved to Rochester, where Jerry became a leading administrator at Mayo Clinic. As he was a strong advocate for Mayo Clinic support for aviation, the main terminal of Rochester International Airport is named in his honor. They raised a son, Mark, and a daughter, Anne. Mark was a banker and real estate appraiser who died in 2009. Anne is a writer in Grand Marais, Minnesota. The Brataases lived on a cul-de-sac at 10½ Street SW with shady gardens where Nancy raised hundreds of varieties of scrupulously labeled hosta and clematis (which she correctly pronounced CLEM-uh-tis). She loved to host garden tours for friends and political associates.

Brataas began her political activism in 1956 as a volunteer in a door-knocking campaign to mobilize voters. She progressed through party ranks to become state chairwoman of the Minnesota Republican Party for three terms in 1963–69; delegate to the Republican National Convention in 1960, 1964 and 1968; then chair of the Minnesota Republican Finance Committee in 1969–71. In 1972, she worked in Washington, D.C., on the campaign to reelect President Nixon. In 1975, Brataas ran in a special election for a seat vacated by Senator Harold Krieger when he was elected as a county judge. She was the second woman elected to the state senate. She liked to note that she was the first woman senator "elected in her own right," as her predecessor was elected to replace her husband, who died in office.

There was no women's restroom in the senate when she started. Other obstacles were numerous. A fierce debater, she overcame obstacles as a woman by being better prepared and more articulate than her opponents. She developed expertise and leadership in education and business, particularly in employment and tax law and in health care. She made major contributions to workers' compensation law, Title IX opportunities for women in sports, a local sales tax to pay for Rochester's massive $100 million–plus flood control project, development of the Federal Medical Center from the abandoned Rochester

State Hospital and work that led to the establishment of the University of Minnesota–Rochester. She was effective in bipartisan efforts despite serving in the minority party throughout her tenure. She was a reliable advocate for equal opportunity for women in all domains. In 1990 and 1992, she was denied the support of her party because of her support for legal abortions. She advocated for Rochester fiercely until 1992, when she retired from the senate. She was succeeded by her good friend Sheila Kiscaden.[140]

While serving in the senate, back in Rochester she managed her political consulting and data-management business, Nancy Brataas Associates Inc. She specialized in get-out-the-vote efforts using technology for voter ID and recruitment campaigns. Her patented system was used throughout the country in political campaigns for Gerald Ford, Ronald Reagan, Texas governor John Connally and others as well as for nonprofit fundraising. In Minnesota, it was key to the election and reelection of Governor Arne Carlson, two U.S. senators and other Republicans. She sold her business in 1981 to Market Opinion Research of Detroit.[141]

After the senate, Brataas served on the Minnesota State Colleges and Universities Board of Trustees, supporting Rochester Community and Technical College and the ultimately successful campaign to establish a branch of the University of Minnesota in Rochester.

I was appointed to the Rochester School Board to fill a vacancy in early 1994 and ran for election that fall. I requested her support for my campaign, and she asked me to present her with my stance on important issues. When I presented her with the twelve to fourteen issues that I considered important, she not only agreed to support me but also offered her political counsel for my campaign. This included help in designing campaign materials and organizing door knocking campaigns along with hours of discussion of campaign strategy. She was a fountain of political wisdom. Once when I was upset about coverage in the local paper, she cautioned me (paraphrasing Congressman Charles Brownson): "Don't get into a war of words with people who buy their ink in 55-gallon drums." We won twice in 1994 and 1997.

In her later years, she traveled extensively, including two round-the-world excursions, once on the *Queen Mary 2* (a luxury cruise ship). In 2012, she decided to give up her consulting business, sell her house and move into a senior living facility. She lived there happily among her many books, artworks and political artifacts.[142] She loved having visitors, particularly political allies. She remained mentally sharp and continued her political discourse with an often-riotous sense of humor. She filed her taxes on time on April 15, 2014, and died two days later on April 17, 2014, at the age of eighty-six.[143]

MAYOR CHUCK HAZAMA, 1978

Chuck Hazama was a popular mayor and an unabashed cheerleader for Rochester. He was elected to eight consecutive two-year terms from 1979 to 1995. His era was noted for tremendous growth and increasing prosperity in Rochester.

He was born on September 1, 1932, in McGerrow Camp in Pu'unene, Maui, Hawaii. He moved to the mainland in 1950 after high school and attended Grinnell College in Iowa until joining the U.S. Army to serve in the Korean War. He received a Purple Heart and was a member of Disabled American Veterans. He returned to the University of Northern Iowa (UNI), received his bachelor's degree in 1957 and continued with graduate studies at UNI.

He married Almira "Aly" Oyakawa in 1958. They had two children, Chuck and Ann. He came to Rochester in 1967 as the physical director at the YMCA and served as executive director from 1972 to 1979.

When the preceding mayor, Alex Smekta, decided not to run for reelection in 1978, Chuck decided to run at the age of forty-six. He was elected and served from 1979 to 1995, sixteen consecutive years. He did not run in 1994— thus, he was never defeated.

Early in his tenure as mayor, he supported the unpopular proposal to establish the Federal Medical Center (FMC) of Rochester. He studied the issue and was convinced that safety concerns regarding escaped convicts were unfounded and that the FMC would provide an economic stimulus to the community through spending for supplies, employment and provision of medical care. His opinion ultimately prevailed, and he remained popular.

Mayor Chuck Hazama. *Courtesy of the Rochester Post Bulletin.*

Mayo Civic Center and Rochester Art Center, south façades, Zumbro River in mid-distance. *Courtesy of Dean Riggott Photography.*

The great flood of 1978 occurred on July 6, well before the election. It was apparent that the new mayor would have a major role in the cleanup and sequelae of the flood. Hazama supported a half-cent sales tax to fund flood control as well as Civic Center expansion. With that citizen-approved levy, he led the flood control project, which raised a total of $134 million and succeeded in controlling the flow of water through the city. The Hazama Memorial on South Broadway at 6th Street acknowledges his leadership.

He played a key role as facilitator of downtown redevelopment in the late 1980s. During his terms as mayor, the city experienced 50 percent population growth, *Money* magazine rated Rochester as the No. 1 place to live in the USA in 1993 and he played a key role in founding Rochesterfest, a weeklong city celebration every June. He also played a key role in initiating Rochester Area Economic Development Inc. to promote business development in Rochester.

Chuck was energetic and service oriented, the "face of the city." He always presented a big smile and firm handshake. He was known for his hospitality and his love of food and travel. In retirement, he and Aly spent winters on Maui and summers in Rochester. He remained popular and a public persona.

He died on November 28, 2021, at the age of eighty-nine at The Waters on Mayowood in hospice care for Alzheimer's disease and a recent stroke.[144]

THE MUSTANGS WIN OLYMPIC HOCKEY GOLD! 1980

The Rochester Mustangs was a semiprofessional hockey team from 1947 to 1970 (American Amateur Hockey League, 1947–52; Central Hockey League, 1952–53; Minnesota Hockey League, 1953–55; U.S. Central Hockey League, 1955–61; United States Hockey League, 1961–70). It was a source of great local hockey and great hockey personalities.

Among the Mustangs' best players was Herb Brooks (1937–2003). He was born in Saint Paul, and his high school team won the 1955 state championship. He played for the University of Minnesota Gophers from 1955 to 1959. He was a member of the U.S. Olympic team in 1960, '64 and '68. Brooks joined the Mustangs in 1961 and played until 1973. In 1962–63, he and Mustangs teammates Ken Johannson and Bill Reichert had the highest scoring forward line in USHL history up to that time. Brooks had a distinguished coaching career, taking the Minnesota Golden Gophers to NCAA championships in 1974, 1976 and 1979. In the 1980 Winter Olympics in Lake Placid, New York, he coached the U.S. "Miracle on Ice" gold medal team. He coached the NHL New York Rangers 1981–85 as well as the Minnesota North Stars (in 1987–88), New Jersey Devils (1992–93) and Pittsburgh Penguins (1999–2000). He also coached the 1998 French Winter Olympic Team in Nagano and the U.S. Olympic team in 2002 in Salt Lake City, defeating Russia in the semifinal game, taking a silver medal after losing in the gold medal game to Canada. He was inducted into the United States Hockey Hall of Fame in 1990 and the International Hockey Hall of Fame in 1999.

Kenneth Johannson, a native of Edmonton, Alberta, played three seasons, 1950–53, for the University of North Dakota in both hockey and football. In hockey, he was the team's leading scorer in 1950–51 and team captain in 1951–53. He played professionally in Europe until joining the Mustangs from 1957 to 1968. He was the Mustangs' leading scorer for three seasons. As player-coach for 1958–60, he led them to the league championship in 1959. During the 1970s, he was national coaching director for the Amateur Hockey Association of the United States. He was general manager of the U.S. national team at the 1979 World Championships and was responsible for the pre-Olympic season and preparation for the 1980 U.S. Olympic hockey team. He resigned as general manager shortly before the Olympics and had cardiac surgery shortly after the Olympics. Meanwhile, Johannson had a day job. From 1959 to 1993, he was a key administrator at Mayo Clinic. Johannson's boss, Robert W. Fleming, chief administrative officer

Left: Ken Johannson in 1976, Mayo Clinic administrator and general manager of the U.S. National Hockey Team for the 1979 World Championships and of the 1980 U.S. Olympic Hockey Team until shortly before the Olympics. *Used with permission of Mayo Foundation for Medical Education and Research.*

Right: Robert Fleming in 1979, Mayo Clinic administrator (later chief administrative officer, 1982–93) and chair of the U.S. Olympic Hockey Committee in 1980. *Used with permission of Mayo Foundation for Medical Education and Research.*

of Mayo Clinic, was also a former Mustang and chair of the U.S. Olympic Hockey Committee from 1969 to 1981 and 1990 to 1994.

The 1980 U.S. Winter Olympic Hockey Team had several additional Rochester connections along with a dominant Minnesota base. For their twenty-player roster, Brooks and Johannson selected twelve Minnesotans, nine from Brooks' Minnesota Golden Gophers, including Rochester native Eric Strobel. All but one of the coaching staff were Minnesotans.[145] The team shared home ice with the Minnesota North Stars, and Brooks and Johannson were well remembered as former Mustangs teammates. Throughout a sixty-one-game pre-Olympic schedule against college, professional and international teams, Johannson made travel arrangements for the team from Rochester, and my mother, who worked for AAA Travel in the subway level of the Mayo Building, was their travel agent for the entire season. The "Miracle on Ice" was savored nationally but nowhere more sweetly than in Rochester.

Lou Nanne is a native of Ontario who played for the Minnesota Gophers in 1960–64. He was drafted by the Chicago Blackhawks but because of a contract dispute played with the Mustangs in 1964–67. He qualified for the U.S. National/Olympic team in 1967–68, after which he signed with the Minnesota North Stars, playing until 1978. He became general manager and coach of the North Stars in 1978 and led them to the NHL playoffs seven consecutive seasons (1979–1986), the Stanley Cup Finals in 1981 and the conference final in 1984. He resigned in 1988 after two losing seasons.

Art Strobel played one season, 1943–44, for the New York Rangers, then for a variety of semi-pro teams in 1944–63, including five seasons with the Mustangs during 1953–63. He coached the Mustangs until 1958, when Ken Johannson succeeded him. Strobel's son, Eric, was a member of the gold medal–winning 1980 U.S. Olympic Hockey Team.

Bill Reichert played for the Mustangs in 1960–69, a linemate with Herb Brooks and Ken Johannson in the high-scoring line of 1962–63. He was captain of the 1964 U.S. Olympic team at the Innsbruck Winter Olympics. He was a high scorer throughout his career and a favorite among Mustangs fans.

The Rochester Mustangs name was revived in 1986 to 2002 by a Rochester-based United States Hockey League team formerly called the Austin (MN) Mavericks. They played at the Rochester Recreation Center and won the American National Junior "A" championship in 1987, 1988 and 1998. The franchise left town after 2002 because of an inadequate facility and poor attendance. Of that era, one of the most notable players was Shjon Podein, a Rochester native, John Marshall High School and University of Minnesota–Duluth graduate who played in the NHL for eleven seasons with the Edmonton Oilers, Philadelphia Flyers, Colorado Avalanche and St. Louis Blues. The Stuart brothers, Mark, Colin and Mike, are from Rochester. Mark and Mike played for the Mustangs, Colin for the USHL Lincoln Stars. All three went on to careers in the NHL. Their father, Dr. Mike Stuart, is a Mayo Clinic orthopedic surgeon and four-time team physician for the U.S. Olympic hockey team (1994, 2010, 2014, 2022).

FERRIS ALEXANDER: THE PORN KING, 1980

Ferris Alexander was the first person in the United States sentenced to jail for pornography violations under the federal racketeering law (RICO). He was convicted in May 1990 of twenty-five counts of racketeering, obscenity and tax fraud. His bookkeeper, Wanda Magnuson, was convicted of similar charges, but his wife and son were acquitted. He appealed all the way to the U.S. Supreme Court, but his convictions were upheld. He was sentenced to six years in prison, and his properties were seized.

He started out selling newspapers in northeast Minneapolis and, between 1970 and 1990, expanded his business to bookstores and theaters presenting sexually explicit materials and movies. By 1975, he and his brother Edward were the top pornography dealers in the Twin Cities. They ran bookstores and theaters in the Twin Cities, Duluth, Winona and Rochester in what some called an "empire of smut."

Like Larry Flynt, Alexander's supporters considered him a defender of free speech. Alexander's attorney Robert Milavitz claimed over one hundred successfully defended free-speech cases in the early 1970s. Another of Alexander's attorneys, Randall Tigue, said, "History will record him as a freedom fighter."

After being convicted, Alexander forfeited all his business assets, including five stores in the 300 block of S. Broadway, Broadway Book I on the east side of the street, Joey's Bookstore and Broadway Video on the west side of the street plus two additional buildings south of Broadway Video that were not open for business. For the period that Alexander was in business, his ownership of much of that block of buildings prevented redevelopment and thus, unintentionally, helped preserve the historic neighborhood. Ironically, that block and the adjacent SW 3rd Street and SW 1st Avenue are now cherished by some as the largest contiguous assembly of vintage commercial properties in the downtown core (see image on page 156).

Alexander died on January 31, 2003, at the age of eighty-four at a nursing home in Excelsior, Minnesota. A World War II veteran, he is buried in Fort Snelling National Cemetery.[146]

Dave Bishop, 1983

David Tyre Bishop was an attorney who represented Rochester in the state legislature for twenty years. As a Republican, he mostly served in the minority party but was successful advocating for Rochester by virtue of his bipartisan efforts backed by towering intellect and pugnacious debating skills, particularly in conference committees at the end of legislative sessions.

He was born on March 9, 1929, in Syracuse, New York, and graduated from nearby Hamilton College in 1951. He received his law degree from

Cornell University Law School in 1954 and a master's degree in public administration from the Kennedy School of Government in 1991.[147]

His wife, Beatrice "Bea" Habberstad, was a native of Rochester, Minnesota. They met at a dance in 1953, and he proposed to her by showing up unannounced while she was studying abroad in Paris. They were married on July 24, 1954, in Rochester, where they lived thereafter. Dave joined the law firm of Furlow, Pemberton and Michaels, practicing family law and becoming a partner in 1956. He was co-chair of the YMCA building committee that raised $1.2 million to build a fifty-thousand-square-foot facility. In 1976, Dave left the law firm to concentrate on real-estate development, eventually owning and managing a large network of commercial and residential properties.

State Representative Dave Bishop at the Minnesota State Capitol. *Courtesy of the History Center of Olmsted County.*

Dave became involved in local Republican politics and in 1982 campaigned for and won an open seat representing Rochester in the state legislature. He kept the position for twenty years. He called himself an Eisenhower Republican and a member of the "bridge-building caucus." He was known for his intellect, depth of knowledge and debating skill as well as his sense of humor. A tall, broad-shouldered man with a deep voice, he could be intimidating and occasionally showed a fiery temperament. In campaign debates, he virtually never complied with speaking time limits.

In the legislature, he represented his district first, his party second. He was moderate or liberal on a variety of social issues, including support for abortion rights. Once, during debate over an anti-abortion bill, he introduced an amendment requiring a man to obtain consent from his wife and parents before a vasectomy.[148]

Dave was a master of bipartisan compromise, particularly when hammered out in the waning hours of legislative sessions by conference committees. According to Lori Sturdevant, retired *Star Tribune* editorial writer and reporter, Bishop was known as a deal maker and "was a popular guy to put on a conference committee…who could find his way forward at a time of partisan division." He wrote a book, titled *Finding Common Ground: The Art of Legislating in an Age of Gridlock*,[149] advocating good faith bipartisanship in service to the needs of the people of the state.

He authored or was responsible for over two hundred bills from 1983 to 2002, described by Sturdevant as "prodigious productivity." He facilitated bills for living wills, sex offender community notification, funding for flood control and local government buildings, tax reduction, living wills, environmental protection and Native American treaty rights, among many others. He had a personal antipathy for highway speed restrictions. He was a member of the minority party until near the end of his tenure. When the Republicans took the majority, he became chair of the House Ways and Means Committee and served in that role for four years until he retired.

In 1995, an informal poll of Minnesota House pages (messengers) ranked him among members of his party "tied for second smartest, second most likely to speak, most liberal, least likely to bow to political expediency, second funniest and member most likely to remain in the Legislature past his 100th birthday."[150]

Bishop retired from public service after the 2002 session (at the age of seventy-three). In retirement, he continued to manage his properties and traveled extensively with his wife. They both loved spending time with their family (five children: Thomas, Kathryn, Marnie Elmer, Lucy, Laura Gallenberger; fifteen grandchildren; fourteen great-grandchildren) at their Round Lake home in Wisconsin.

I was a member of an investment club for many years with Dave. He was a knowledgeable and enthusiastic investor. Far more than other club members, he frequently made recommendations for investments to consider. Many of his recommendations were received positively, but not all. Once he proposed a new stock, but his motion to consider it failed for lack of a second. It triggered his temper, and he shouted an expletive at the group and stormed out. Twenty minutes later a member of the club arrived late and asked, "Why is Bishop out pacing up and down the sidewalk?" He had forgotten that he had gotten a ride with one of the other members. It was too far to walk, and he didn't have his cellphone, so he had to wait for a ride home. He remained a member of the club, and nothing was said about the incident thereafter.

Dave and Bea lived at Charter House for their last several years. Dave died at the age of ninety-one on August 3, 2020. Bea followed him just four months later at the age of eighty-nine on December 6, 2020, after sixty-six years of marriage.

THE FEDERAL MEDICAL CENTER (FMC), 1984

From 1879 until 1982, the Second Minnesota Hospital for the Insane, later called Rochester State Hospital (RSH), provided care for citizens of the state, mostly indigent, who suffered from mental illness. In partnership with Mayo Clinic, RSH also functioned as the sole surgical referral center for the entire state hospital system, as well as the Department of Public Welfare. In 1981, the Minnesota legislature ordered Rochester State Hospital to be closed as a "cost-saving" measure, regardless of the superior care coordinated with Mayo Clinic. Despite protests, the hospital closed in June 1982.

The vacated campus did not sit empty for very long. In 1984, the Federal Medical Center (FMC) of Rochester (at 2110 East Center Street) was established as a federal prison hospital by the Federal Bureau of Prisons, reusing part of the former RSH campus. Other buildings outside the FMC facility are used for Olmsted County Public Health Services, planning and other county offices. The FMC houses up to 711 male inmates of any security status, some as hospital patients, other as general inmates.[151]

Prior to the sale, there was considerable debate in the community regarding the pros and cons of the FMC. Safety concerns related to possible

Public entrance to the Federal Medical Center (FMC) Rochester. *Courtesy of the History Center of Olmsted County.*

breakouts or criminal elements infiltrating the community were balanced against the economic benefit of jobs provided. The public support of then mayoral candidate Chuck Hazama and the quiet support of Mayo Clinic contributed to the ultimate decision in favor of the facility. Since the facility was established, there has been one escape: thirty-four-year-old inmate David A. Wieling, who walked away from an outside work detail on August 8, 1995. He was apprehended a year later in a farmhouse in Iowa and was eventually released in 2008.

Well-known current residents include: (1) Jared Lee Loughner, serving a life sentence, without parole, for the 2011 Tucson, Arizona shootings of U.S. Representative Gabby Giffords and the murder of six other people, including U.S. District Judge John Roll; (2) Luke Helder, the Midwest Pipe Bomber, now 42 years old, being held indefinitely for planting homemade pipe bombs in mailboxes in five midwestern states in 2002. He was ruled incompetent to stand trial in 2004. (3) Louis "Bobby" Manna is a 93-year-old former high-ranking member of the Genovese Mafia family in New Jersey sentenced to eighty years in prison in 1989 for conspiring to murder John Gotti, his younger brother Gene Gotti and Irwin "Fat Man" Schiff in aid of racketeering. Enigmatic big spender Schiff was shot in the head in an expensive Manhattan restaurant by a masked gunman who was never identified. Recent requests for release of Manna have been denied. He is scheduled for release on November 7, 2054, at age 124.

Previous inmates include (1) Sheikh Omar Abdel-Rahman, "The Blind Sheikh," an Egyptian cleric convicted of seditious conspiracy related to the 1993 World Trade Center bombing and for plotting simultaneous bombings at the headquarters of the United Nations, the FBI field office in Manhattan and two commuter tunnels linking New York and New Jersey. He was also convicted of plotting to kill Egyptian president Hosni Mubarak. He died in custody while serving a life sentence in 2017 after transfer to another facility in Butner, North Carolina. (2) Dennis Hastert, former Illinois Republican congressman (1987–2007) and speaker of the U.S. House of Representatives (1999–2007), pleaded guilty to breaking financial rules regarding hush money aimed at covering up his sexual abuse of teenagers when he was a high school wrestling coach. He served thirteen months out of a fifteen-month sentence in 2016–17. (3) Lyndon LaRouche was a perennial U.S. presidential candidate from 1976 to 2004 as either a Democrat or a Socialist. He was convicted in 1988 of scheming to defraud the IRS and deliberately defaulting on more than $30 million in loans from his supporters. He served five years out of a fifteen-year sentence and was released in 1994. (4) Leonard Peltier, American Indian Movement leader, has been serving life imprisonment since 1977 for participating in a shootout that resulted in the deaths of two FBI agents. He was transferred to the Rochester FMC in 2000 to be close to Mayo Clinic for treatment of diabetes, a heart condition and a jaw condition. He is now in Belcourt, North Dakota. Recent requests for parole have been denied. (5) Jim Bakker, televangelist founder of Praise the Lord Ministries (PTL), was convicted of fraud in 1989 for stealing millions of dollars in donations from his members. He was released in 1994 after serving five years. (6) Dan Rostenkowski, former Illinois Democrat U.S. congressman (1959–95), chair of House Ways and Means Committee, pleaded guilty in 1996 to mail fraud in the Congressional Post Office Scandal and served seventeen months in prison. (7) Gregory Scarpa was also known as the "Grim Reaper," a hit man for Colombo crime family (Mafia) of New York City and FBI informant. He died in custody in 1994 in Rochester while serving a life sentence for three murders. (He was suspected of over 100 murders.) (8) James Traficant, former Ohio Democrat U.S. congressman, was sentenced in 2002 to seven years in prison for taking bribes, filing false tax returns, racketeering and forcing staff to do private work for him. (9) Vito "Billy Jack" Giacalone was a capo or team captain of the Detroit Mafia, a prime suspect in the 1975 disappearance of Teamsters leader Jimmy Hoffa. He pleaded guilty to tax evasion charges in 1994. He died in prison in Clinton, Michigan, never having revealed his secrets, in 2012 at the age of eighty-eight. (10) Robert "Bob" Probert was a Canadian NHL hockey "enforcer" left wing for the Detroit Red Wings (1985–94) and Chicago Blackhawks (1995–2002). He was arrested in 1989 for transporting fourteen grams of cocaine across the Canada/U.S. border. He served three months in federal prison in Rochester, Minnesota, as a general nonmedical inmate, then three more months in a halfway house. While in the FMC, he roomed with Bakker, whom he described as "kind of wimpy…always complaining," and Giacalone, of whom he said, "He was really cool." He was reinstated into the NHL and had a surprisingly long career for an enforcer. At retirement, he was the fourth most penalized NHL player with 3,300 penalty minutes. In twenty-one years, he scored 384 points in 935 games played. He died in 2010 of a heart attack at the age of forty-five. Examination of his brain showed evidence of chronic traumatic encephalopathy.[152]

RONALD REAGAN, 1989

Mayo Clinic employees are prohibited from discussing patients with members of the public because of patient confidentiality rules. However, some celebrity incidents occur in public and are publicized nonetheless, such as former president Ronald Reagan's famous half-bald "hats off" salute as he boarded his plane leaving Rochester following treatment for a subdural hematoma.

Ronald and Nancy Reagan were patients of Mayo Clinic during and after President Reagan's term in office. Nancy's father, Dr. Loyal Davis, was a faculty advisor to Mayo surgeon Dr. Oliver Beahrs when Beahrs was a medical student at Northwestern University Medical School in Chicago. Nancy was a teenager when she and Beahrs first met. During and after President Reagan's term in office (1981–89), Dr. Beahrs introduced the Reagans to a number of colleagues who participated in their medical dare, including Dr. Ron Peterson, who participated in Mr. Reagan's care for Alzheimer's disease.[153]

In 1989, the year he left office, President Reagan came to Mayo Clinic for a routine checkup. He was discovered to have a subdural hematoma next to his brain, which was attributed in retrospect to a fall from his horse. It was treated successfully at St. Mary's Hospital. As he recovered and was leaving Rochester, his departing shaved-head wave was caught by *Post Bulletin* photographer Merle Dalen and distributed internationally.[154]

President Ronald Reagan waving to well-wishers at Rochester International Airport. *Photo by Merle Dalen; courtesy of the* Rochester Post Bulletin.

KING HUSSEIN OF JORDAN, 1999

King Hussein of Jordan had several prolonged stays in Rochester near the end of his life (1935–1999). He was a military pilot who flew his own royal transport, a Lockheed 1011 jumbo jet with the Jordanian flag on the tail. His presence in town was always obvious because of his jet parked on the tarmac at the airport. He was known to enjoy driving his favorite vehicle, a Volkswagen Beetle, exploring the countryside of southeast Minnesota. One evening, at the Executive Terminal of the Rochester Airport, a Gulfstream G700 private jet arrived and discharged its lone passenger, Harrison Ford. He walked through the lobby, graciously signing autographs and posing for pictures with numerous admirers, eventually walking out to the curb to be picked up by a Volkswagen Beetle driven by his friend King Hussein, whom he dropped in to visit.[155]

MAYOR ARDELL BREDE, 2003

Ardell Brede (pronounced Brady) served as mayor of Rochester for sixteen years from January 6, 2003, to January 7, 2019. He succeeded eight-year incumbent mayor Chuck Canfield, whom he defeated as a political newcomer with 55 percent of the vote in his favor. His long term in office was characterized by 26 percent growth in the population with increasing prosperity in the city and rejuvenation of the downtown. The increasing diversity, and acceptance of diversity, in the populace has largely taken place during his tenure. He played a key role in promoting legislation for Destination Medical Center as well as in its early implementation.

He was the unfailing face of the city, attending, by his count, an average of over 1,300 events per year, including most home Honkers games and most cultural events. An unapologetic cheerleader for the city, when asked, he was always prepared to deliver a few words of welcome with an amusing anecdote or two. He was renowned for his unfailing support for Minnesota Gopher athletics and his love of official travel representing the city nationally and internationally. He also was known for his office full of teddy bears, to which some claim he bears a strong resemblance.

Brede is a native of Austin, Minnesota, born on June 23, 1939. He received an associate degree in commerce from the Austin Junior College in 1959 and took additional courses through the University of Minnesota Extension Division and Brigham Young University.

Mayor Ardell Brede. *Courtesy of the* Rochester Post Bulletin.

He was employed by Rochester Methodist Hospital until the merger with Mayo Clinic in 1986, after which he was employed by Mayo Clinic until retiring in 2002 shortly after being elected mayor. He served Methodist and Mayo in numerous roles, including admissions, business services, systems and information support and finance administration. He was a member of the Mayo Clinic Historical Committee in the 1980s and 1990s and referred to the committee as "the conscience of the institution." He loves historical anecdotes.

As mayor, Brede's enthusiastic support for the arts was acknowledged by the Greater Rochester Arts & Cultural Trust and the arts community, first by naming their annual excellence awards, the Ardee Awards, after him. Secondly, their entire program in 2018 was staged as a tribute to the outgoing mayor.

Mayor Brede served in leadership roles with the League of Minnesota Cities and the U.S. Conference of Mayors. He was active as a lobbyist at the state legislature not only for Rochester but for outstate Minnesota in general. He was honored by the Coalition of Greater Minnesota Cities (CGMC) in 2018 for excellence in service to Greater Minnesota with its Jack Murray Award. He was acknowledged for his active leadership of CGMC and his effective lobbying at the state legislature during his years as mayor of Rochester (Greater Minnesota's largest city). He served on the

Coalition's Board of Directors and as co-chair of its media committee. Dave Smiglewski, mayor of Granite Falls and president of the CGMC, described him as "one of our most enthusiastic and passionate leaders."

He married his wife, Judith "Judy" Ellen Nelson Brede, later a registered nurse, on March 24, 1961. She, too, retired from Mayo and reveled in her unofficial role as Rochester's first lady, regularly accompanying Ardell to events, as she loved to travel with him representing the city. After fifty-seven years of marriage and a lengthy struggle with dementia, she died on November 27, 2018. Ardell was devoted to her and visited her daily. They have three children: Leslie Kennedy, Scott Brede and Jennifer Brede.

Brede is politically unaffiliated but has endorsed several prominent Democrats and favors a liberal approach to voting laws. He chose not to run for reelection in 2018 and was succeeded by Mayor Kim Norton, Rochester's first woman mayor.[156]

Igor Vovkovinskiy (1982–2021), 2009

The tallest man in American called Rochester his home. Igor Oleksandrovych Vovkovinskiy was born on September 18, 1982, in Bar, Ukraine, to Svetlana Vovkovinska and Oleksandr Ladan. Early in childhood, he developed a pituitary tumor that secreted excessive growth hormone. He weighed eleven pounds at birth and was six feet tall by the age of six. His mother, Svetlana, sought care for him at Mayo Clinic, where his tumor was partly removed, but it continued to secrete growth hormone throughout his life. He and Svetlana stayed for needed medical care. He was a graduate of John Marshall High School (2000), where he played basketball, and Rochester Community and Technical College. He dreamed of becoming a lawyer and took paralegal classes at Minnesota School of Business. He grew to 7 feet, 8⅓ inches (234.5 centimeters), making him the tallest living person in the United States. He lived with Svetlana in a house specially built to accommodate his height and weight. Svetlana is an ICU nurse at Mayo Clinic.

Igor admired President Barack Obama. He attended political rallies wearing a T-shirt printed with "World's Biggest OBAMA Supporter." President Obama acknowledged him at Target Center in 2009: "The biggest Obama fan in the country is in the house—I love this guy....He's a great supporter and it's great to see you here." They shook hands and were photographed together after Obama's speech.

Igor Vovkovinskiy with new shoes. *Courtesy of the* Rochester Post Bulletin.

He also dreamed of being an actor. In 2007, he was featured in a documentary *Inside Extraordinary Humans: The Science of Gigantism*. In 2011, he had a cameo role in the movie *Hall Pass*. He visited the set and, in a surprise move, was invited by the director to film a bar scene. He met the stars of the show: Owen Wilson, Jason Sudekis, Jenna Fischer and Christina Applegate. In May 2013, he appeared in the Eurovision song contest in Malmo, Sweden. He carried the Ukrainian entry, Zlata Ognevich, onto the stage (in front of an estimated television audience of 125 million). He wore an elaborate costume paired with her fairy costume. In 2016, he appeared on the *Dr. Oz Show* in New York City and was certified by Guinness World Records as the tallest living man in America. He was featured on a fourteen-minute segment of *60 Minutes Australia* in 2018 describing his life and its challenges, concisely summarized as "the loneliest man in the world."

Igor endured many hardships related to his height. His basketball career was cut short by a stress fracture in his foot and a fractured elbow from a fall. After early childhood, he lacked properly fitting clothes and shoes. As an adult, he received specially made size 26 EEEEEEEEEE shoes from Shaquille O'Neal and from Reebok, but by that time his feet were severely damaged from ill-fitting shoes. He had many orthopedic procedures on his damaged feet. He drove a car with a specially placed seat and controls. Despite chronic suppressive medications, the excess growth hormone took its toll in other ways. He was diabetic and developed heart disease. Igor died at the age of thirty-eight of heart failure on August 20, 2021, at St. Marys Campus of Mayo Clinic Hospital in Rochester. Mike Dougherty spoke for those who knew Igor in his memorial article: "We are sad with Igor's passing. He was a good guy." He quoted Igor from a 2016 interview: "Really count your blessings. Really appreciate all of the little things you have."[157]

Half a year after Igor's death, Russia invaded Ukraine. Igor's older brother, Oleh Ladan, was traveling to London on business when he heard the news. He did not hesitate to travel to Ukraine to join a volunteer battalion that successfully defended Kyiv from the invaders. He now volunteers as a civilian to support logistics of transport of military goods. He speaks strongly in support of Ukrainian culture and independence: "[Putin] says we're brothers. There's nothing wrong with being neighbors. But we're not brothers."[158]

I look in the mirror now.
I see that time can be unkind.
But I know every wrinkle.
And I earned every line.
So, wear it like a royal crown
When you get old and gray.
It's the cost of living.
And everyone pays.

—*Don Henley,* The Cost of Living, *Cass County*

NOTES

I. Early Days

1. Guthrie, "Medicine and Its Practitioners," 2, 3. This lengthy essay was published serially in *Minnesota Medicine*, 1949–51, and subsequently republished as a 212-page monograph, presumably by Mayo Foundation.
2. Severson, *Rochester*, 26.
3. Brewer, *Trails of a Paintbrush*, 37.
4. Severson, *Rochester*, 19.
5. Leonard, *History of Olmsted County*, 268.
6. Eaton, *History of Winona and Olmsted*, 922; Upham, *Minnesota Place Names*, 386.
7. Severson, *Rochester*, 29.
8. Raygor, *Rochester Story*, 139.
9. Gregory and Hyuck, "God Help America," 44–58 (ranking of "Most Annoying States" in which Minnesota ranked no. 31).
10. Upham, *Minnesota Place Names*, 413–17. Little Valley Cemetery is 4.5 miles east of MN 42 on County Road 2 (east of Viola, south of Elgin); Farm Hill Cemetery is 200 yards east of U.S. Highway 63 on 125th Street NE; Ringe Cemetery is 2 miles east of U.S. Highway 63 on 75th Street NE; Othello Cemetery is 2.7 miles west of Genoa on County Road 14; Cline (Plank's/Laird's) Cemetery is 2.5 miles south of Eyota, 0.2 mile west on 55th Street.
11. Leonard, *History of Olmsted County*, 276.

12. Andreas, *Illustrated Historical Atlas*, 117.

13. Harold Knapp and his wife, Iva, had three sons: Harold Cowles Knapp (1914–2013), Richard W. Knapp, DDS (1918–2015) and Willard Knapp (1920–????). Richard was a local dentist. Willard was locally renowned as a perennial candidate for elective office. He objected to elections with only one candidate, so he made a regular practice of filing to run against anyone unopposed. He was elected only once, as justice of the peace in the 1980s. Shortly after he was elected, the office was abolished by the city council, a decision he supported. He was also the publisher and editor of the *Queen Citian*, a short-lived Rochester magazine that premiered on August 11, 1968.

14. Leonard, *History of Olmsted County*, 102, 145, 148, 166, 194–95, 263, 270, 279, 281, 285; Eaton, *History of Winona and Olmsted*, 772–74; "Milling Firm Liquidates; Industry Determined Site of Rochester Due to Power," *Post Bulletin*, March 21, 1930; Sean Kettelkamp, "The Olds Mill Reservation" (unpublished manuscript, February 2021); Hahn, Lost Rochester, 29–33, 35–38; "Lake Florence Missed by Young and Old," *Post Bulletin*, March 7, 1994; historic plaque re: Alexander's Woolen Mill in Slatterly Park by bicycle path just south of 6th Street SE; "NewsMD, A Mill on the Zumbro," *Post Bulletin*, November 5, 2013; Upham, *Minnesota Place Names*, 389.

15. Leonard, *History of Olmsted County*, 156, 195, 409; Eaton, *History of Winona and Olmsted*, 934–35; obituary, Walter L. Brackenridge, *Post and Record*, December 15, 1899.

16. Olmsted County property records, History Center of Olmsted County.

17. *Rochester Post*, June 30, 1866.

18. Leonard, *History of Olmsted County*, 60, 279; Severson, *Rochester*, 135, 210; Eaton, *History of Winona and Olmsted*, 646; *Minnesota in the Civil and Indian Wars*, 126, 128, 718; *Rochester Post*, July 22, 1876, October 21, 1876, December 7, 1877, July 16, 1886; Hilgendorf, "From Heaney Block"; location of burial site from Find a Grave.

19. Brewer, *Trails of a Paintbrush*.

20. L'Enfant, *Nicholas R. Brewer*.

21. *Olmsted County Democrat*, August 9, 1901, cited in Petersen and LaBrash, *History of the Rochester Fire Department*, 343.

22. Allsen, *Old College Street*, 80–82; Leonard, *History of Olmsted County*, 165.

23. Leonard, *History of Olmsted County*, 215, 218–20; Eaton, *History of Winona and Olmsted*, 1032; Scanlon, *Rochester Stories*, 80–82; George Healy biography, *Daily Record* (date unknown); George Healy obituary, *Record and Union*, August 14, 1896; George Healy obituary, *Rochester Post*, August 14,

1896; "The Library Accepts $5000," *Olmsted County Democrat*, November 7, 1895; "Admitted to Probate," *Olmsted County Democrat*, September 24, 1896; Allsen, *Master Architect*, 50.

24. "Proceedings in Memory of Former Justice Start, April 30, 1920," *Minnesota Reports* 144 (1920): 1–21, https://mncourts.libguides.com/ld.php?content_id=63295684.

25. Weber, "Early Rochester City Attorney"; Leonard, *History of Olmsted County*, 100, 302.

26. "Civil War (M–Z Index) Medal of Honor Recipients," U.S. Army Medal of Honor, https://www.army.mil/medalofhonor/citations2.html; "John Vale: 1835–1909," Minnesota Medal of Honor Memorial, https://www.minnesotamedalofhonormemorial.org/wp-content/uploads/2017/12/Vale-John-Bio-June-16.pdf; Weber, "Three Medal of Honor Recipients"; Congressional Medal of Honor Society, https://www.cmohs.org.

27. Together with architect Clarence Johnston, they built the Chapel of St. Mary of the Angels (1924), the convent (Alverna Hall, 1925), the power plant (1928) and a dormitory (Lourdes Hall, 1929).

28. Leonard, *History of Olmsted County*, 136, 242, 442; Allsen, *Old College Street*, 86; Allsen, "Academy of Our Lady of Lourdes" (monograph prepared for the Franciscan Sisters of Rochester, Minnesota, June 18, 2019); Ken Allsen, "College of St. Teresa Architectural History" (monograph prepared for the Franciscan Sisters of Rochester, Minnesota, May 3, 2019); Martin Heffron obituary, *Rochester Post Bulletin*, September 15, 1938.

29. Marek, "Part One."

30. Leonard, *History of Olmsted County*, 232–33, 274, 562–63; Andreas, *Illustrated Historical Atlas*, 119; "Landmarks and Historic Districts," Minneapolis: City of Lakes, https://www2.minneapolismn.gov.

31. Allsen, *Old College Street*, 67–69, 87; Scott, "Bridge Builder of Olmsted County."

32. Eaton, *History of Winona and Olmsted*, 667–85.

33. Obituary, *Rochester Post and Record*, December 22, 1899.

34. "Assisi Heights and the Wilson House," Mayo Clinic Heritage & History, https://history.mayoclinic.org; "About Us," Sisters of Saint Francis, https://rochesterfranciscan.org; "Franciscan Sisters," Religions in Minnesota, https://religionsmn.carleton.edu; "Assisi Heights: Motherhouse and Monument, Welcome to Rochester," *Post Bulletin*, March 14, 1997; brochure commemorating seventy-fifth anniversary of the Sisters of St. Francis, May 28, 1952; brochure from dedication of Assisi Heights Motherhouse, March 31, 1955; Russell, "Partnership Keeps

Assisi Intact"; Sonnenberg, "Motherhouse of Sisters of St. Francis"; Allsen, "Assisi Heights Architectural History" (monograph prepared for the Franciscan Sisters of Rochester, Minnesota); Allsen, "Academy of Our Lady of Lourdes"; Allsen, "College of St. Teresa."

35. Howard, "Rise and Fall of Sears"; Weber, "Sears Store Entered the Market."

36. Leonard, *History of Olmsted County*, 260; *Olmsted County Historical Society Monthly Bulletin*, August 1958, 69–71.

37. "A Brief History of the Conley Camera Co.," http://sevenels.net/Conley/history.html.

38. Severson, *Rochester*, 280–81.

39. "Company Has History of Varied Products," *Post Bulletin*, February 29, 1992.

40. Freund, "Waters Instruments Ponders New Name."

41. Waters Medical Systems, https://wtrs.com/.

42. "Brief History of the Conley Camera Co."

43. Setterholm, "History Buff?"

44. Ernest H. Maass Sr., "Autobiography of Ernest H. Maass, Sr." (unpublished manuscript); Maass and McAndrews Company building, historic preservation certification application, Section 6, statement of significance, 12, 13; Stevenson Williams and Jane Bisel, Maass and McAndrew Company Building historic preservation certification application, Reference No. 16000278.

45. Setterholm, "New Life for Historic Rochester."

46. Williams and Bisel, Maass and McAndrew Company Building.

47. Bleu Duck, https://www.bleuduckkitchen.com/about.

48. "Collider Coworking Announced as Location for First Google Office in Minnesota," Collider, https://www.collider.mn/.

49. Leonard, *History of Olmsted County*, 253–54.

50. Severson, *Rochester*, 102–4.

51. "Byron Killer-Bandit Shoots Self," *Rochester Post Bulletin*, September 7, 1933.

52. *Post Bulletin*, March 16, 17, 18, 26 and 27, 1971.

53. Robert John Ryan, Appellant, v. United States of America, Appellee, 547 F.2d 426 (8th Cir. 1977), Justia US Law, https://law.justia.com.

54. Severson, *Rochester*, 108–9.

55. "Rochester Man Sentenced 8 Years for Bank Robbery," *Post Bulletin*, October 6, 1992.

56. "Suspected Sterling State Bank Robber Runs by KIMT News 3 Reporter Adam Sallet on Live TV," YouTube, https://www.youtube.com.

57. Nelson, *Mayo Roots*, 140–41; Harwick, *Forty-Four Years*, 15–16.

58. Clapesattle, *Doctors Mayo*, 592.

59. Richards and OCHS Staff, *Olmsted County Historical Society*; Leonard, *History of Olmsted County*, 153; Clapesattle, *Doctors Mayo*, 164, 211, 379-381, 541, 545, 592.

60. Wilson, "Method for the Rapid Preparation," 1,737.

61. *Physicians of the Mayo Clinic*, 1485–91; Allsen, *Century of Elegance*, 62, 96; Allsen, *Houses on the Hill*, 113.

62. Clapesattle, *Doctors Mayo*, 709.

63. Nelson, *Mayo Roots*, 168, 298–305; Wright-Peterson, *Women of Mayo Clinic*, 81–88, 163–68.

64. Nelson, *Mayo Roots*, 242–43.

65. *Sketch of the History*, 101.

66. Clapesattle, *Doctors Mayo*, 532; Wright-Peterson, *Women of Mayo Clinic*, 88–90; "A Mayo 'Pioneer' Reaches 100," *Mayovox*, February 1978, 1,4, 5; Mayo Historical Unit file 0675, Interview with Mabel Root, Daisy Plummer and Fredrick Willius, October 1960.

67. Harwick, *Forty-Four Years*.

68. Clapesattle, *Doctors Mayo*, 524, 527, 529, 532, 591.

69. Herrell, "Physician-Administrator P," 107–9; Boutelle, *Oronoco Past and Present*; Strobel, "Harwick Lake Shady Home."

70. "Mayowood," Society for Architectural Historians, https://sah-archipedia.org; National Register of Historic Places application for Pill Hill Historic District, Rochester, Minnesota, October 22, 1900; Allsen, *Old College Street*, 85–86; *Post and Record*, April 23, 1909/.

71. Scott, "Mayo Park Had Zoo."

72. "Answer Man," *Post Bulletin*, May 19, 2016; William Befort obituary, *Post Bulletin*, September 14, 1960; "Answer Man," *Post Bulletin*, November 4, 2009.

73. Unless otherwise noted, grave site locations were obtained from findagrave.com.

74. "Moonlight Graham," Wikipedia, https://en.wikipedia.org; "Dr. Archibald Wright 'Moonlight' Graham," Find a Grave, https://www.findagrave.com; *The Real Moonlight Graham: A Life Well Lived*, Mayo Heritage Films, c. 2001–2021; "Chisholm Medic, 83, Posts 100th Trip to Mayo Clinic," *Post Bulletin*, August 14, 1961.

II. Between the Wars

75. Allsen, *Houses on the Hill*; Allsen, *Master Architect.*
76. The Reunion at Rochester, Minnesota, event program, October 14, 1916; History of the Rochester Old School Boys and Girls Association, 1927; Know Rochester, Official Program: Sixth Reunion of Old Boys and Girls of Rochester, August 17, 18, 19, 1941; Eaton, *History of Winona and Olmsted*, 731–39.
77. Allsen, Old College Street, 54–57; Allsen, *Century of Elegance*, 194; Weber, "College Apartments."
78. Hahn, *Hidden History of Rochester*, 107–12; Mayo Clinic Archives, Correspondence of Cooper to WJ Mayo, May 1, 1916, WJM Papers, Box 083.
79. Severson, *Rochester*, 181–90; "History," Rochester Public Utilities, https://www.rpu.org/about-rpu/history.php.
80. "Woman Suffrage," National Geographic, https://education. nationalgeographic.org.
81. Hahn, Hidden History, 87–97; "Votes for Women," Minnesota Historical Society, https://www.mnhs.org.
82. Raygor, *Rochester Story*, 116.
83. Molseed, "Did You Know."
84. Leonard, *History of Olmsted County*, 215–16.
85. Halliwell, "50 Years of Beer."
86. Wasson, "Bootleggers Made Southeast Minn."
87. Hanson, "State View."
88. Worcester, "Last Chance Liquor."
89. Johnson, *Mayo Clinic*, 21.
90. "$100,000 Fire Destroys Laboratory," *Post Bulletin*, May 8, 1923.
91. David Block, "Institute Hills Farm" (unpublished history, October 1994).
92. *Sketch of the History*, 73–91.
93. *Twenty-Fifth Anniversary.* This is an internally published and distributed brochure in celebration of the twenty-fifth anniversary of Mayo Foundation's Institute of Experimental Medicine. The author has a copy, also accessible from Mayo archives.
94. *Mayovox* 2, no. 13 (1951): 1–3; "'Institute Hills Farm' New Title Given to Institute of Experimental Medicine," *Mayovox* 6 no. 6 (1955); Wilder, "Mayo Clinic," 42; Nelson, *Mayo Roots*, 188.
95. Else, "Day in History."

96. Lund, "Rochester Women Paved Path"; *Post Bulletin*, October 20, 1971; History Center of Olmsted County, "Belva Snodgrass," Facebook, September 1, 2020, https://www.facebook.com/OlmstedHistoryCenter/posts/belva-snodgrass-teacher-dean-of-students-director-of-student-accounting-and-15-y/10157895818894263/.

97. "Answer Man," *Post Bulletin*, January 16, 2018.

98. Leonard, *History of Olmsted County*, 223.

99. Scott, "Game of Checkers"; "City Bequeathed $50,000 in Property by Williams Will; Park Playgrounds to Benefit," *Rochester Post Bulletin*, May 20, 1932; Freeberg, "City Parks Kept Lively"; Frank E. Williams obituary, *Rochester Post Bulletin*, May 21, 1932; Hilgendorf, "Frank Williams Left His Mark."

100. *Monarch Finer Foods*, promotional brochure by Reid, Murdoch & Co., accessible from History Center of Olmsted County archives; "15 Million Cans with Rochester Label Shipped to All U.S. Sections Annually," *Post Bulletin*, May 2, 1938.

101. Scanlon, *Rochester Stories*, 131; Severson, *Rochester*, 283.

102. Weber, "Unique Chapter in Rochester History"; Lucy Wilder obituary, *Post Bulletin*, July 15, 1968; Riffel, "Feminist Viewpoint"; Taub, "Profiles: Close to the Sun."

103. A History of the Whitewater Watershed in Minnesota, http://www.whitewaterwatershed.org/wp-content/uploads/2017/01/Whitewater-Watershed-Conservation-History_Minnesota.pdf.

104. Minnesota Division of Isaak Walton League of America, https://www.minnesotaikes.org/Izaak/History.html.

105. Albert J. Lobb, "The Rochester Airport" (undated memoir), Mayo Clinic Archives, MHU 0676. Airports (RST) Subject File.

106. Hilgendorf, "Big Aircraft Repair Service."

107. Hilgendorf, "Welcome to Rochester"; Hilgendorf, "How Many Area Airports?"; Lee Hilgendorf, personal communication.

108. Helmholz, "C. Anderson Aldrich," 669–74; Nelson, "Historical Profiles of Mayo," 496; "Nursery School Set Up by Aldrich Was Revolutionary, Spock Says," *Post Bulletin*, April 29, 1995; Aldrich School, https://aldrichschool.com/history/.

109. Comroe, "Pay Dirt," 957–68.

III. Modern Times

110. Harwick, *Forty-Four Years*, 1, 2.

111. Scanlon, *Rochester Stories*, 155–56; Dougherty, "Sign of the Times," 9.

112. "Claude Henry McQuillan," FamilySearch, https://ancestors. familysearch.org; Scanlon, "Black Experience in Rochester"; "45 Mayors. 160 Years," *Post Bulletin*, January 11, 2019, https://www.postbulletin. com; "John Marshall High School (Minnesota)," Wikipedia, https:// en.wikipedia.org; Else, "Alderman McQuillan Becomes a Candidate."

113. "Pappas Brothers Head to Hospitality Hall of Fame," *Post Bulletin*, October 17, 1994; Reilly, "Rochester's Michael's Restaurant Closes"; Hendrickson, "Pappas Family Celebrates 75 Years"; James Pappas obituary, *Post Bulletin*, October 30, 1993; Charles Pappas obituary, *Post Bulletin*, February 6, 2018.

114. Severson, *Rochester*, 282–83: Kiger, "Heard on the Street"; "Crenlo," Datanyze, https://www.datanyze.com.

115. Asians in Minnesota, Oral History Project, Minnesota Historical Society, interview with Michael Hong Wong, 1979, https://media.mnhs. org/things/cms/10219/306/AV1981_361_13_M.pdf.

116. Severson, *Rochester*, 286–90; "Olmsted Medical Center's History," Olmsted Medical Center, https://www.olmmed.org; "How One Physician's Practice Grew to Be a Regional Leader in Community Care: Faces of Homestead Medical Center," Med City Beat, August 31, 2021, https://www.medcitybeat.com; Snyder, "Olmsted Medical Group."

117. Reprinted with permission from email written by G. Slade Schuster Jr., to PDS, March 10, 2023.

118. Roy Watson Jr. obituary, Ranfranz & Vine Funeral Homes, https:// www.ranfranzandvinefh.com; "Roy Watson, Rochester Business and Parks Leader Dies," *Post-Bulletin*, September 11, 2012; Roy Watson obituary, *Star Tribune*, September 12, 2012; Else, "Roy Watson Sr."; Severson, *Rochester*, 89, 91, 128; Underwood, *Colonial House*, 140–43.

119. The following account is as published by State Representative Dave Bishop (D.T. Bishop, "Why IBM Came to Rochester," *Post Bulletin*, October 15, 2011), a longtime neighbor and family friend of Lester Fiegel Jr., and as corroborated by members of the Fiegel family and other sources as cited. Answer Man was not fully convinced by the sources available (Answer Man, *Post Bulletin*, September 27, 2022). He concluded, saying, "The bottom line is that neither the archivists at IBM and Mayo Clinic nor the Rochester Public Library's amazing reference librarian

Susan Hansen or even the Answer Man's crack investigative team could find definitive proof that the Watson/Fiegel friendship brought IBM to Rochester. It's still a good story." A follow-up was published on October 8, 2022, noting further evidence for the connection received from Leland's sister, Audrey Fiegel Higgins Garbish. Answer Man concluded: "So there is proof that friendship did bring a Fortune 500 company with a massive facility and thousands of jobs to Rochester in the 1950s."

120. Based on comments at dedication of Lester J. Fiegel Sr. Memorial by Audrey Fiegel Higgins Garbish, August 14, 2021; "Lester John Fiegel," FamilySearch, https://ancestors.familysearch.org; correspondence from Scott Leland Fiegel; "Farm Boys on Broadway," *Post Bulletin*, April 2, 1936.

121. "General Returns from Mission to Moscow," *Rochester Post Bulletin*, December 2, 1942.

122. "Fiegel Flies Bomber Here, Weds and Returns to Base," *Rochester Post Bulletin*, April 16, 1942.

123. Watson and Petre, *Father, Son & Co.*, 96–109.

124. *Foreign Relations of the United States*, Diplomatic Papers, 1942, Europe, Volume III, 607n5, https://history.state.gov/historicaldocuments/frus1942v03/pg_607.

125. "Shastakovich's Seventh," *Life* magazine, November 1942.

126. "General Bradley Stops Over Here," *Rochester Post Bulletin*, December 3, 1942.

127. "Distinguished Flying Cross Awarded to Major Fiegel," *Rochester Post Bulletin*, March 13, 1943; Letter of Commendation from Major General E.J. Timberlake Jr., May 11, 1945, from Fiegel family archives.

128. Topper, "Town Toppers."

129. Bishop, "Why IBM Came"; "IBM Head Flew in War with Late Col. Fiegel," *Rochester Post Bulletin*, undated 1956 clipping re: announcement of new plant; "Watson Urges MMS Grads to Put Patient First," *Mayovox*, June 1987; "Answer Man, Is a Rochester Legend about a Wartime Friendship and IBM Really Accurate?" *Post Bulletin*, September 27, 2022; "Answer Man, IBM CEO Chose to Build Rochester as a Tribute to His Friend," *Post Bulletin*, October 8, 2022.

130. "Lester Fiegel [Sr.], Retired Banker, Dies at Age 85," *Rochester Post Bulletin*, November 18, 1969; Lester J. Fiegel, Jr. obituary, Legacy, https://www.legacy.com.

131. Klecker, "Former Minnesota Supreme Court Chief Justice"; Jahns, "Sandy Keith Remembered."

132. Butterfass, "Hemingway."

133. Ibid.; Rosengren, "Last Days of Hemingway"; Jahns, "Hemingway's Final Chapter."

134. By permission from Stapleton Kearns.

135. Johnson, *Mayo Clinic*, 128.

136. Rocca et al., "History of the Rochester Epidemiology Project," 1,202–13; Melton, "History of the Rochester Epidemiology Project," 266–74.

137. Judy Onofrio, 2005 McKnight Distinguished Artist, http://judyonofrio.com; Silberman, "Stuff of Art," 40–43, 64.

138. "Answer Man," *Post Bulletin*, August 24, 2007.

139. Senator Brataas's daughter, Anne Brataas, maintains a website (www.nancybrataas.org) with additional information and insightful tributes by friends and admirers.

140. "Hughes, Brataas Won't Run."

141. "Brataas Selling Firm to Major U.S. Pollster," *Post-Bulletin*, August 14, 1981.

142. Carlson, "Brataas Defies the Odds."

143. Brataas, "As She Died"; Nancy Brataas obituary, *Post-Bulletin*, April 18, 19, 2014.

144. Chuck Hazama obituary, *Post-Bulletin*, December 4, 2021; Stolle, "Chuck Hazama Was a Cheerleader"; "Hazama Left Lasting Lessons for Local Leaders," *Post-Bulletin*, December 4, 2021, anonymous editorial.

145. The 1980 U.S. Olympic Team, U.S. Hockey Hall of Fame, https://www.ushockeyhalloffame.com.

146. "Alexander Convicted of 25 Felony Charges," *Post-Bulletin*, May 24, 1990; "Ferris Alexander Dies at 84," *Post-Bulletin*, March 3, 2003; "Ferris Jacob Alexander," Find A Grave, https://www.findagrave.com/memorial/27245687/ferris-jacob-alexander.

147. David Bishop obituary, *Post-Bulletin*, August 2020; David Bishop obituary, *Star Tribune*, August 16, 2020.

148. Stolle, "Dave Bishop Was Someone Who Could Find the Way Forward," *Post-Bulletin*, August 11, 2020.

149. Bishop, *Finding Common Ground*.

150. McCormick, "Pages Run Bishop."

151. Scanlon, *Rochester Stories*, 49–51.

152. "Federal Medical Center, Rochester," Wikipedia, https://en.wikipedia.org; Stolle, "Mobsters, Terrorists, Disgraced Politicians"; Rochester Federal Medical Center, MN, Nationwide Inmate Records Online Checks, https://gadsdensheriff.org/minnesota/federal/rochester-federal-medical-center/.

153. Sparks and Dacy, "In the Loop"; "Reagans Planning Mayo Clinic Visit," *Post-Bulletin*, August 9, 1989.
154. "Classic Shot: President Reagan," *Post-Bulletin*, November 20, 2013, https://www.postbulletin.com.
155. Witnessed by Alan O. Tuntland.
156. Pieters, "Brede Bunch Waves"; Coalition of Greater Minnesota Cities announcement, Rochester Mayor Ardell Brede receives Jack Murray Award from CGMC, July 30, 2018; "Mayor Brede Deserving MVP," Rochester Sports, September 11, 2018, https://www.rochestermnsports.org; Weber, "Brede Honored at Annual Ardee Awards."
157. Igor Vovkovinskiy obituary, *Post-Bulletin*, May 24, 2021; Lange, "Count Your Blessings"; Olson, "Nation's Tallest Man"; Lange, "America's Tallest Man"; Stolle, "Fighting for Ukraine."
158. John Marshall graduate Oleh Ladan on war in native Ukraine: "I get angry and want to do more," *Post Bulletin*, January 17, 2023.

SOURCES

Allsen, Ken. "Academy of Our Lady of Lourdes Architectural History (1877–1955)." Monograph Prepared for the Franciscan Sisters of Rochester, Minnesota, June 18, 2019 (2nd revision February 6, 2020).

———. "Assisi Heights Architectural History (1955–)." Monograph prepared for the Franciscan Sisters of Rochester, Minnesota (draft version, 2022).

———. *A Century of Elegance: Ellerbe Residential Design in Rochester, Minnesota.* Minneapolis, MN: Ellerbe Beckett, 2009.

———. "College of St. Teresa Architectural History (1884–1989)." Monograph prepared for the Franciscan Sisters of Rochester, Minnesota, May 3, 2019 (3rd revision February 16, 2021).

———. *Houses on the Hill: The Life and Architecture of Harold Crawford.* Kenyon, MN: Noah Publishing, 2003.

———. *Master Architect: The Life and Works of Harold Crawford.* Rochester, MN: History Center of Olmsted County, 2014.

———. *Old College Street: The Historic Heart of Rochester, Minnesota.* Charleston SC: The History Press, 2012.

Andreas, A.T. *An Illustrated Historical Atlas of the State of Minnesota.* Chicago: A.T. Andreas, 1874.

Bishop, David T. *Finding Common Ground: The Art of Legislating in an Age of Gridlock,* Minnesota Historical Society Press, 2015

———. "Why IBM Came to Rochester." *Post-Bulletin,* October 15, 2011.

Boutelle, Elsie. *Oronoco Past and Present.* Zumbrota, MN: Sommers Printing Inc., 1983.

Brataas, Anne. "As She Died, Sen. Nancy Brataas Posed a Final Question: 'Unconventional?'" *MinnPost*, April 25, 2014.

Brewer, N.R. *Trails of a Paintbrush: An Artist's Memoir*. Minneapolis–St. Paul, MN: Afton Press, 2021.

Butterfass, Dan. "Hemingway." *Post-Bulletin*, July 4, 2001.

Calavano, Alan. Postcard History Series: *Rochester*. Charleston, SC: Arcadia Publishing, 2008.

Carlson, Heather J. "Brataas Defies the Odds, Former State Senator Passes 6-Month Mark, Doctor's Predictions." *Post-Bulletin*, August 30, 2013.

Clapesattle, Helen. *The Doctors Mayo*. Minneapolis: University of Minnesota Press, 1941.

Comroe, Julius H., Jr. "Pay Dirt: The Story of Streptomycin, Part II. Feldman and Hinshaw; Lehmann." *American Review of Respirator Disease* 117, no. 5 (1978): 957–68.

Dougherty, Mike. "Sign of the Times: How One Mayor Fought (Literally) the City's Racists." *Rochester Magazine*, November 2004.

Eaton, Samuel William. *History of Winona and Olmsted Counties*. Chicago: H.H. Hill, 1883.

Else, Loren. "Alderman McQuillan Becomes a Candidate for Rochester Mayor." *Post-Bulletin*, January 7, 2022.

———. "Day in History." *Post-Bulletin*, October 20, 2021.

———. "Roy Watson Sr., Retired Kahler Chief, 76, Dies." *Post-Bulletin*, September 7, 2016.

Freeberg, Ron. "City Parks Kept Lively by Quiet Man's Bequest." *Post-Bulletin*, n.d.

Freund, Bob. "Waters Instruments Ponders New Name." *Post-Bulletin*, September 30, 2005.

Gregory, Alex, and Peter Hyuck. "God Help America." *Spy*, May/June 1996.

Guthrie, Nora H. "Medicine and Its Practitioners in Olmsted County prior to 1900." *Minnesota Medicine* 32 (1949), 33 (1950), 34 (1951): 2, 3.

Hahn, Amy Jo. *Hidden History of Rochester Minnesota*. Charleston, SC: The History Press, 2022.

———. *Lost Rochester Minnesota*. Charleston, SC: The History Press, 2017.

Halliwell, Anne. "50 Years of Beer at Schuster Brewing Company." *Rochester Magazine*, *Post-Bulletin*, March 9, 2018.

Hanson, David J. "State View: Why Minnesotans Came to Despise Prohibition." *Duluth News Tribune*, October 6, 2008.

Hartzell, Judith. *I Started All This: The Life of Dr. William Worrall Mayo*. Greenville, SC: Arvi Books, 2004.

Harwick, Harry J. *Forty-Four Years with the Mayo Clinic: 1908–1952*. Rochester, MN: Mayo Clinic, 1957.

Helmholz, H.F. "C. Anderson Aldrich (1888–1949)." *Journal of Pediatrics* 47, no. 5 (1955): 669–74.

Hendrickson, Wayne. "Pappas Family Celebrates 75 Years at the Hubbell House." *Dodge County Independent*, June 23, 2021.

Herrell, John H. "The Physician-Administrator Partnership at Mayo Clinic." Mayo Clinic Proceedings 76 (2001): 107–9.

Hilgendorf, Lee. "Frank Williams Left His Mark on Rochester." *Post-Bulletin*, February 24, 2020.

———. "Lens on History: Big Aircraft Repair Service in a Small Town." *Post-Bulletin*, November 23, 2021.

———. "Lens on History: From Heaney Block to Horton Block." *Post-Bulletin*, June 20, 2021.

———. "Lens on History: How Many Area Airports?" *Post-Bulletin*, October 31, 2017.

———. "Lens on History: Welcome to Rochester, Minnesota." *Post-Bulletin*, May 7, 2018.

Howard, Vicki. "The Rise and Fall of Sears." *Smithsonian Magazine*, July 25, 2017.

Hughes, John. "Brataas Won't Run Again." *Post-Bulletin*, July 21, 1992.

Jahns, Isaac. "Hemingway's Final Chapter: A Look Back at the Writer's time at Mayo Clinic." *Med City Beat*, April 14, 2021.

———. "Sandy Keith Remembered as a Leader Who 'Cared Enormously about Helping People.'" *Med City Beat*, October 5, 2020.

Johnson, Victor. *Mayo Clinic: Its Growth and Progress*. Voyageur Press, 1984.

Kiger, Jeff. "Heard on the Street: Rochester's Crenlo Sells Off Its Emcor Enclosures Division." *Post-Bulletin*, October 11, 2021.

Klecker, Mara. "Former Minnesota Supreme Court Chief Justice Sandy Keith Dies." *Star-Tribune*, October 5, 2020.

Lange, Steve. "America's Tallest Man, and a Heavy Weight." *Rochester Magazine*, October 2021.

———. "Count Your Blessings, Igor Told Us." *Post-Bulletin*, August 24, 2021.

L'Enfant, Julie. *Nicholas R. Brewer: His Art and Family*. Edina, MN: Afton Press, 2019.

Leonard, Joseph A. *History of Olmsted County Minnesota*. Chicago: Goodspeed Historical Association, 1910.

Lund, Bryan. "Rochester Women Paved Path to Power with Organization, Education. *Med City Beat*, March 25, 2022.

Marek, Patrick. "Part One—Blood on the Altar." *Winona Post*, October 24, 2001.

McCormick, John. "Pages Run Bishop to the Top in Their Poll." *Post-Bulletin*, May 26, 1995.

Melton, L.J. "History of the Rochester Epidemiology Project." *Mayo Clinic Proceedings* 71, no. 3 (1996): 266–74.

Minnesota in the Civil and Indian Wars. St. Paul, MN: Board of Commissioners, 1890.

Mitchell, W.H. *Geographical and Statistical History of the County of Olmsted, Together with a General View of the State of Minnesota, from Its Earliest Settlement to the Present Time*. Rochester, MN: Shaver & Eaton, 1866.

Molseed, John. "Did You Know Prohibition Got Its Start Here?" *Post-Bulletin*, January 17, 2020.

Monarch Finer Foods, Time Tells the Story: 90ᵗʰ Anniversary Edition. Reid, Murdoch & Co., 1942.

Nelson, Clark W. "Historical Profiles of Mayo: Dr. Benjamin M. Spock and Mayo." *Mayo Clinic Proceedings* 73 (1998): 496.

———. *Mayo Roots: Profiling the Origins of Mayo Clinic*. Rochester, MN: Mayo Foundation for Medical Education and Research, 1990.

Olson, Rochelle. "Nation's Tallest Man Made Home in Rochester." *Star Tribune*, August 23, 2021.

Petersen, Minard, Betty LaBrash and Elmer LaBrash. *History of the Rochester Fire Department: 1866–2000*. Minneapolis: University of Minnesota Printing Services, 2000.

Physicians of the Mayo Clinic and the Mayo Foundation. Minneapolis: University of Minnesota Press, 1937.

Pieters, Jeffrey. "Brede Bunch Waves in New Rochester Mayor." *Post-Bulletin* (Austin edition), November 6, 2002.

Post-Bulletin (Rochester, MN), archives dating from 1856.

Raygor, Mearl W. *The Rochester Story*. Rochester, MN: Schmidt Printing, 1976.

Reilly, Mark. "Rochester's Michael's Restaurant Closes after 63 Years." *Minneapolis/St. Paul Business Journal*, January 2, 2015.

Richards, Carolyn, and OCHS Staff. *The Olmsted County Historical Society: The 1ˢᵗ 75 Years—1926 to 2001*. Merchants Bank, 2001.

Riffel, Marlise. "Feminist Viewpoint; Lucy Wilder's Spirit Alive and Well in Memories." *Post-Bulletin*, June 22, 1988.

Rocca, Walter A., et al. "History of the Rochester Epidemiology Project: Half a Century of Medical Records Linkage in a US Population." *Mayo Clinic Proceedings* 87 (December 2012): 1,202–13.

Rosengren, John. "The Last Days of Hemingway at Mayo Clinic, Mpls." *St. Paul Magazine*, March 2019.

Russell, Matt. "Partnership Keeps Assisi Intact." *Post-Bulletin*, November 16, 2009.

Scanlon, Paul D. "The Black Experience in Rochester, A Brief History." *Post-Bulletin*, July 9, 2021.

———. *Rochester Stories: A Med City History*. Charleston, SC: The History Press, 2021.

Scott, Cindy. "Lens on History: A Bridge Builder of Olmsted County." *Post-Bulletin*, January 6, 2015.

———. "Lens on History: A Game of Checkers Helps Kids." *Post-Bulletin*, June 8, 2010.

———. "Lens on History: Mayo Park Had Zoo into 1940s." *Post-Bulletin*, February 5, 2013.

Setterholm, Andrew. "History Buff? Tour Conley-Maass Building Tonight." *Post-Bulletin*, September 18, 2015.

———. "New Life for Historic Rochester Building." *Post-Bulletin*, December 8, 2015.

Severson, Harold. *Rochester: Mecca for Millions*. Rochester, MN: Marquette Bank & Trust, 1979.

Silberman, Robert. "The Stuff of Art: Judy Onofrio." *Americana Craft* 56, no. 3 (June/July 1996).

Sketch of the History of the Mayo Clinic and the Mayo Foundation. Philadelphia: W.B. Saunders Company, 1926.

Snyder, Karen L. "Olmsted Medical Group and Olmsted Community Hospital." *Post-Bulletin*, April 1, 1994.

Sonnenberg, Marietta. "Motherhouse of Sisters of St. Francis Nears Completion." *Post-Bulletin*, March 23, 1955.

Sparks, Dana, and Matt Dacy. "In the Loop: Remembering Nancy Reagan and a 'Magical Friendship.'" Mayo Clinic News Network, March 10, 2016. https://newsnetwork.mayoclinic.org.

St. Mane, Ted. *Rochester, Minnesota*. Charleston, SC: Arcadia Publishing, 2003.

Stolle, Matthew. "Chuck Hazama Was a Cheerleader, a Leader." *Post-Bulletin*, December 4, 2021.

———. "Dave Bishop Was Someone Who Could Find the Way Forward." *Post-Bulletin*, August 11, 2020.

———. "Fighting for Ukraine: Oleh Ladan Volunteers in Battle against Russia." *Post-Bulletin*, January 16, 2023.

———. "Mobsters, Terrorists, Disgraced Politicians, and Televangelists: The Famous and Infamous Who Have Been Imprisoned at Rochester's Federal Medical Center. During Its 36-Year Operation, the FMC Has Housed Many Notable Characters." *Post-Bulletin*, December 1, 2021.

Strobel, Nancy. "Harwick Lake Shady Home 'Modern,' but Reflects Past." *Post-Bulletin*, August 15, 1963.

Taub, Ben. "Profiles: Close to the Sun." *New Yorker*, October 10, 2022.

Topper, B.W. "Town Toppers." *Post-Bulletin*, June 13, 1964.

Twenty-Fifth Anniversary of the Institute of Experimental Medicine, 1924–1949. Rochester, MN: Mayo Foundation for Medical Education and Research, 1949.

Underwood, Francis H. *The Colonial House Then and Now.* Rutland, VT: Charles E. Tuttle Company, 1977.

Upham, Warren. *Minnesota Place Names, a Geographical Encyclopedia.* 3rd ed. Minnesota Historical Society Press, 2001.

Wasson, Mark. "Bootleggers Made Southeast Minn. a Prohibition Hotspot." *Post-Bulletin*, October 15, 2022.

Watson, Thomas J., Jr., and Peter Petre. *Father, Son & Co., My Life at IBM and Beyond.* New York: Bantam Books, 1990.

Weber, Thomas. "Brede Honored at Annual Ardee Awards Event. AP News, October 25, 2018.

———. "Early Rochester City Attorney Climbed State's Legal Ladder." *Post-Bulletin*, November 16, 2021.

———. "Sears Store Entered the Market when Rochester Was at a Crossroads." *Post-Bulletin*, April 5, 2022.

———. "Then and Now: The College Apartments Were Rochester's Original 'Luxury apartments.'" *Post-Bulletin*, October 20, 2020.

———. "Then and Now: A Unique Chapter in Rochester History. Two Bookstores Led the Way Downtown in the 1930s and '40s." *Post-Bulletin*, January 3, 2021.

———. "Three Medal of Honor Recipients Have Loose Links to Rochester." *Post-Bulletin*, September 21, 2021.

Wilder, Lucy. *The Mayo Clinic.* New York: Harcourt, Brace & Company, 1938.

Wilson, L.B. "A Method for the Rapid Preparation of Fresh Tissues for the Microscope." *Journal of the American Medical Association* 45, no. 23 (1905): 1737.

Worcester, Mike. "Last Chance Liquor 'til South Dakota, County Option in Minnesota 1915–1965." *Minnesota History* 68, no. 2 (Summer 2022).

Wright-Peterson, Virginia M. *Rochester: An Urban Biography*. St. Paul: Minnesota Historical Society Press, 2022.

———. *Women of Mayo Clinic: The Founding Generation*. St. Paul: Minnesota Historical Society Press, 2016.

INDEX

ABOUT THE AUTHOR

Paul David Scanlon, MD FACP, FCCP, is professor emeritus of medicine in the Division of Pulmonary and Critical Care Medicine at Mayo Clinic, Rochester, Minnesota. He trained at the University of Minnesota (bachelor of arts in humanities, cum laude, 1975), Mayo Medical School (MD, 1978), Johns Hopkins (internal medicine, 1978–81) and Harvard (pulmonary and critical care medicine, 1981–84). He was a member of the staff of Mayo Clinic in Rochester for thirty-five years (1984–2019). He served as medical director of the Mayo Clinic Pulmonary Function Laboratories, the busiest such laboratory in North America, for thirty years (1988–2018). He was the founding medical director of the Mayo Clinic Pulmonary Clinical Research Unit (1994–2019). He was the medical director of the Mayo Clinic Dolores Jean Lavins Center for Humanities in Medicine (2003–18). He was a member of the Mayo Clinic Historical Committee for thirty years and served as committee chair in 2001–3. Scanlon is author or coauthor of over one hundred peer-reviewed scientific articles, as well as book chapters and editorials and a popular book on pulmonary function interpretation, now in its fifth edition. He is the senior author of the original descriptions of the nonspecific pattern and the complex restrictive pattern, which were previously unrecognized and, together, account for 15 percent of all complete pulmonary function tests. He was a practicing clinician in pulmonary and critical care medicine and active in clinical trials of therapies for chronic obstructive pulmonary disease (COPD) and asthma, as well as studies of pulmonary physiology and new developments in pulmonary function testing. He served as a consultant for important environmental issues, including asbestos hazards in Libby, Montana, and the Minnesota Taconite Workers Health Study of asbestos-related diseases. He taught regularly in the medical school, ICU, clinic and pulmonary function laboratory. He retired from clinical practice on November 13, 2019.

Scanlon was born at St. Mary's Hospital. His Mayo Clinic medical record number starts with a 1. He has lived in Rochester all but nine years of his life. He is actively engaged in the community, having served as president of Rochester Public Schools Board of Directors, president of Rochester Montessori School Board of Directors, president of the Rochester Art Center Board, vice president of the Rochester Civic Music Board and president of the Rochester Park Board. He is currently board president for the History Center of Olmsted County. He and his wife, Maggie, a retired nurse, have three children, a computer guru and two nurses, and seven grandchildren. His hobbies include cycling, skiing, kayaking, arts and architecture, antiques and local politics. He is a collector of antiques and memorabilia, particularly books and postcards related to Rochester, Minnesota, and Mayo Clinic. He is the author of *Rochester Stories: A Med City History* (The History Press, 2021).

Visit us at
www.historypress.com